# CROWN, CROSS, AND "FLEUR-DE-LIS"

# STANFORD
# FRENCH AND ITALIAN
# STUDIES

*editor*

ALPHONSE JUILLAND

*editorial board*

ROBERT GREER COHN

RAYMOND D. GIRAUD

JOHN C. LAPP

PAULINE NEWMAN-GORDON

*assistants to the editors*

KAMAL ZEIN

LAURIE EDSON

*volume VI*

ANMA LIBRI

# CROWN, CROSS, AND "FLEUR-DE-LIS"

**AN ESSAY ON PIERRE LE MOYNE'S BAROQUE EPIC "SAINT LOUIS"**

## WILLIAM CALIN

1977

ANMA LIBRI

*Stanford French and Italian Studies* is a collection of scholarly publications devoted to the study of French and Italian literature and language, culture and civilization. Occasionally it will allow itself excursions into related Romance areas.
*Stanford French and Italian Studies* will publish books, monographs, and collections of articles centering around a common theme, and is open also to scholars associated with academic institutions other than Stanford.
The collection is published for the Department of French and Italian, Stanford University by Anma Libri.



LC 76-42318
ISBN 0-915838-34-6

## *Foreword*

The reader may wonder why a medievalist chooses to write on an obscure baroque epic. My previous work was concerned largely with long narrative poems of the Middle Ages, primarily late *chansons de geste* (*The Old French Epic of Revolt*, 1962; *The Epic Quest*, 1966) and the love-allegories of Guillaume de Machaut (*A Poet at the Fountain*, 1974). It became apparent to me that in the Middle Ages the major genres—*chanson de geste, roman courtois*, and *dit amoureux*—form a continuity of epos. The medieval period gives the lie to the Voltairean cliché "Les Français n'ont point la tête épique"; in fact, the long poem dominates the first three centuries of French literary history, and it is from France that her neighbors (Spain, Italy, Germany, England) learned to sing of heroism and romance in the vernacular.

I am currently engaged on a more ambitious project, a study of the long poem from the Middle Ages up to the twentieth century. Suffice it to say, whereas in the period extending from Ronsard to Chénier writers generally accepted the theoretical supremacy of the Virgilian *poëme heroïque*, in practice the long poem was never to dominate esthetically the literary production of that age or the subsequent one: it yielded precedence to the lyric, the tragedy, and finally the novel. Nonetheless, some of the greatest masters of French literature have practiced the mode, in its serious and comic forms, and with extraordinary success: I am thinking of d'Aubigné, Saint-Amant, Boileau, Voltaire, Lamartine, Hugo, Saint-John Perse, Aragon, and Pierre Emmanuel. Their work proves that epic seeds are solidly, fruitfully planted in Gaul, have flowered in the last four centuries, and need hardly dread comparison with the production of Italy or the British Isles.

Under these circumstances I came across the works of Pierre Le Moyne. In spite of laudatory remarks by Jean Rousset and some good recent criticism (see below pp. 12-13), this extraordinary baroque master remains largely unknown to scholars in French literature; he is but a name even to the majority of *dix-septiémistes*, and his poetry has not been re-edited for the last three hundred years. For these very reasons, I believe that Le Moyne's epic has a claim to more extensive treatment than one out of eighteen or twenty chapters in a synthesis on the long poem in France, and that the reader deserves copious quotations to be able to savor the tone and texture of *Saint Louis* without recourse to a seventeenth-century folio. It is true, because many a baroque poet has been rehabilitated since Boas' discovery of Sponde, it is now a temptation and pitfall of our profession to write on obscure authors no one else has "covered" and, of necessity, to claim great things for them. My hope is that Pierre Le Moyne truly merits the attention I and others are now granting him, that he stands apart from those who sometimes serve as a pretext for rehabilitation.

In terms of methodology, I shall employ both traditional and modern critical approaches. I am interested in problems such as the influence of Tasso, ideological values, typology, attitudes toward history, the treatment of women, spatial and temporal patterns, romance archetypes, imagery, and elements of the baroque. As a medievalist, I can hardly bring myself to condemn startling metaphor, nonmimetic characters and episodes, and a plot not constructed with the rigor people are accustomed to find in Racine and Flaubert. It is quite possible that the history of literature itself evolves according to a cyclical pattern, therefore that certain baroque writers—du Bartas, d'Aubigné, La Ceppède, Théophile, Saint-Amant, and Le Moyne, among others—are closer in spirit to the Middle Ages and to the centuries of romanticism and surrealism than to Boileau and La Bruyère. This may explain why our age, in resolutely anti-classical fashion, continues to rehabilitate these formerly despised *attardés* and *égarés*, and why the tools of modern criticism—Freudian, Jungian, phenomenological, and structuralist—are eminently appropriate for such purposes. We the children of surrealism perhaps represent the ideal public for a Pierre Le Moyne, capable of appreciating his strengths and of forgiving his failings.

# Contents

# 1 The French Epic in the Seventeenth Century: An Overview

Quantitatively, if not qualitatively, the seventeenth century is one of the great periods in the history of the French epic. One scholar provides us with over 100 titles of heroic poems; another insists that only fifty of these can be considered true epics.[1] Be this as it may, the number of long poems, whether 46, 118, or a compromise figure in between, corresponds favorably to the epic production of the early Middle Ages and was surpassed only in the time of Lamartine and Hugo. Within the century the flowering of epic can be assigned to two main periods. Between 1600 and 1610, eleven epics were written. Many of these were composed at the court of Marguerite de Valois. They include four imitations of, or sequels to, *La Franciade*. Unfortunately, all eleven are failures. Of more interest are the heroic poems composed between 1653 and 1671. In the 1650s six highly regarded poets published epics. These are: Saint-Amant's *Moÿse sauvé* (1653); Scudéry's *Alaric* (1654); Godeau's *Saint Paul* (1654); Chapelain's *La Pucelle* (1656); Desmarets de Saint-Sorlin's *Clovis* (1657); and Le Moyne's *Saint Louis* (1658). Another thirteen or so came to life in the succeeding decade, including four Biblical narratives by Jacques de Coras, and a *Marie-Madeleine* (1669) and an *Esther* (1670) also by Desmarets. However, they are relatively modest, sober, and, above all, short and thus manifest a reaction against the long heroic poem; they bear witness to decline in the genre.

The epics of the 1650s appeared on the literary scene at the

---

[1] Raymond Toinet, *Quelques Recherches autour des poèmes héroïques-épiques français du dix-septième siècle*, 2 vols. (Tulle, 1899-1907); Archimede Marni, *Allegory in the French Heroic Poem of the Seventeenth Century* (Princeton, 1936), pp. 3, 105.

same time as the madrigal. Do they embody the typically "baroque" heroism of the age? or a nostalgic yearning for absent heroism? or are they a literary phenomenon, come into being from strictly literary causes? It is certain that the writers of epic gave expression to a nostalgia for power and glory, for honor, heroic living, and knightly doings, but also that the nobility tried to live up to such models of heroism in their own lives. In this period, as in the twelfth century, heroic literature reflects and helps create wish-fulfillment on the part of a threatened aristocratic class. So also do comparable literary manifestations: the great prose romances, *Le Grand Cyrus* and *Clélie*, and the last heroic plays of Corneille: *Andromède* (1650), *Don Sanche d'Aragon* (1650), *Nicomède* (1651), and *Pertharite* (1653). To some extent, *Alaric* and *Clovis* as well as *Cyrus* and *Andromède* bridge the gap between epic and romance, between heroism and gallantry, as did, four and one-half centuries earlier, late *chansons de geste* such as *Huon de Bordeaux* and *Renaud de Montauban*. Since, however, the majority of the Homers and Tassos of the 1650s began to write during the reign of Louis XIII, under the sway of Richelieu, this particular literary manifestation ought to be associated with the age as a whole, not the specific, highly localized incidents of the Fronde (1648-1653). We might also consider literary forces that encouraged epic production: Jesuit instruction in the colleges; the example of Italy—of Tasso's *Gerusalemme liberata* and a host of *seicento* imitations—as well as of Ronsard, Du Bartas, and the abortive epics of Henry IV's reign; and, finally, a reaction on the part of certain social classes, literary circles, and individual poets against the frivolous court-lyrics of Voiture and his circle, and the esthetics of moral gallantry and oblique licentiousness they represent.

With the succeeding generation the epic ceased to be in vogue, due in part to the striking failure of *La Pucelle* (the purported masterpiece that people had been awaiting for so many years), in part to the savage attack on the French epic school contained in Boileau's *Art poétique* (1674), in part to a far-reaching shift in taste, from what we now call the baroque to the classical age. It is also true that most of these poems are pompous, rigid, tediously correct, and sterile. Their creators sought to instruct rather than please, to inspire virtue at all costs, always a dangerous wish in art. And they were guilty of a mechanical adherence to the "rules" of epic production as laid down by Tasso, Castelveltro, Piccolomini, Scaliger, Vida, and Vossius. These poems all contain armed, casked maidens, seductive sorceresses, enchanted islands or palaces, Satanic magicians, council scenes in hell and heaven, lengthy foretelling of the patron's genealogy, and so on. A distinguished scholar echoes the generally accepted opinion when he states: "En fait, aucune de ces œuvres n'est encore lisible. Aucune ne mérite même le plus timide effort de réhabilitation."[2] Although, on the whole, I agree with Adam's formulation, I wish to make two exceptions. These are Saint-Amant's *Moÿse sauvé* and Le Moyne's *Saint Louis*, in my opinion literary works of the highest quality, deserving careful, loving scrutiny. Their only fault is to have come into the world at a time of shifting esthetic taste, surrounded by a host of mediocre brothers, sisters, and cousins. Le Moyne's poem will form the subject of this essay.[3]

---

[2] Antoine Adam, *Histoire de la littérature française au XVIIe siècle*, Vol. 2 (Paris, 1951), p. 65.

[3] On the seventeenth-century epic in France, consult Julien Duchesne, *Histoire des poëmes épiques français du XVIIe siècle* (Paris, 1870); P.V. Delaporte, *Du Merveilleux dans la littérature française sous le règne de Louis XIV* (Paris, 1891); Toinet, *Quelques Recherches autour des poëmes héroïques-épiques*; Ralph Coplestone Williams, *The Merveilleux in the Epic* (Paris, 1925); René Bray, *La Formation de la doctrine classique en France* (Paris, 1927); Marni, *Allegory in the French Heroic Poem*; Daniel Mornet, *Histoire de la littérature française classique, 1660-1700* (Paris, 1940); Adam, *Histoire de la littérature française*; R.A. Sayce, *The French Biblical Epic in the Seventeenth Century* (Oxford, 1955); Simone Noehte, *Moyse Sauvé von Saint-Amant: Ein Beitrag zu Konzeption und Stil des christlichen Epos in Frankreich um die Mitte des 17. Jahrhunderts* (Frankfurt am Main, 1962); Antoine Adam, *L'Age classique: I. 1624-1660* (Paris, 1968); David Maskell, *The Historical Epic in France, 1500-1700* (Oxford, 1973).

## 2   *Presenting Pierre Le Moyne*

Among serious, "important" writers of the seventeenth century, Pierre Le Moyne, S.J., is one of the most obscure. He is among the few whose works we have to consult in the original folio editions,[4] a man totally unknown to the general reading public in France and even to the majority of professors. The baroque period, more even than the Middle Ages, suffered from neglect on the part of scholars that has only recently been corrected. Indeed, it is in the last generation or so that specialists in seventeenth-century studies have rediscovered a number of poets—Sponde, La Ceppède, and Chassignet, in the first rank; Fiefmelin, Poupo, Labadie, Auvray, Hopil, Du Bois Hus, and Drelincourt in the second—so that the period extending from Ronsard to La Fontaine can now be revalued as one of the richest in the history of French verse. No man has contributed more to this revaluation than Jean Rousset, author of the major study on the French literary baroque and editor of an important anthology of baroque poetry.[5] Rousset quotes extensively from Pierre Le Moyne and refers to him as an extraordinarily gifted writer, the Victor Hugo of his century. (It is also true that Rousset limits his praise to Le Moyne the lyricist and considers *Saint Louis* to be his worst book.)

[4] The only exception being extracts from Le Moyne's *Dissertation du poëme heroïque* printed in *Dichtungslehren der Romania aus der Zeit der Renaissance und des Barock*, ed. A. Buck, K. Heitmann, and W. Mettmann (Frankfurt am Main, 1972), pp. 459-465. I shall quote from my copy of *Les Œuvres poétiques du P. Le Moyne* (Paris: Thomas Jolly, 1672), an edition less inaccessible than the others; I intentionally retain the seventeenth-century orthography and punctuation.

[5] Jean Rousset, *La littérature de l'âge baroque en France: Circé et le paon* (Paris, 1953); *Anthologie de la poésie baroque française*, 2 vols. (Paris, 1961); also, "L'eau et le soleil dans le paysage des poètes," *Cahiers de l'Association Internationale des Études Françaises*, 6 (1954), 49-55; "Un Brelan d'oubliés," *L'Esprit Créateur*, 1 (1961), 91-100; and "Les eaux miroitantes," *Baroque*, 3 (1969), 7-14.

12

As to be expected, prior to 1950 research devoted to Le Moyne proves to be meagre indeed, limited mostly to brief comments in books on the seventeenth-century epic as a whole or to Tasso's influence in France, and to articles in provincial antiquarian journals. Two notable exceptions stand out from the rest: Henri Chérot, *Étude sur la vie et les œuvres du P. Le Moyne (1602-1671)*,[6] a solid, voluminous work, dated in terms of literary criticism but indispensable for any one interested in Le Moyne's biography and an excellent introduction to his opus as a whole; and Nathan Edelman, *Attitudes of Seventeenth-Century France toward the Middle Ages*,[7] an excellent book of literary history containing a sympathetic, intelligent chapter on "National Heroes and Heroic Poetry" in general, and Le Moyne's epic in particular. Since Rousset, two studies have appeared: Esther Gross-Kiefer, *Le Dynamisme cosmique chez Le Moyne*,[8] a Swiss doctoral dissertation written under the direction of Georges Poulet and influenced especially by Poulet's *Les Métamorphoses du Cercle*; and Solveig Schult Ulriksen, "Pierre Le Moyne—poète baroque français"[9] (a résumé of a 1965 Norwegian doctoral thesis by Asbjørn Aarnes, *Pierre Le Moyne: En fransk barokkdikter*). I also wish to mention David Maskell, *The Historical Epic in France 1500-1700* (see note 3 above), a revised Oxford Ph.D. dissertation which contains perceptive remarks on Le Moyne. This present monograph is the first piece of modern criticism devoted exclusively to *Saint Louis, ou la Sainte Couronne reconquise*. I hope that, along with the writings of Rousset, and the three dissertations, it will call attention to the quite extraordinary literary production of this French Jesuit and lead to a modern edition of his opus so that he will soon come to occupy his rightful place as one of the great poets of the age.

Pierre Le Moyne wrote a vast quantity of religious verse and prose. Among his works largely or exclusively in prose are *Les Peintures morales* (1640 and 1643); *La Gallerie des femmes fortes* (1647), his most popular book, translated into English, Italian, and German; *La Devotion aisée* (1652), a treatise in the line of

---

[6] Paris, 1897.
[7] New York, 1946.
[8] Zurich, 1968.
[9] *Orbis Litterarum*, 25 (1970), 19-40.

Francis of Sale's *Introduction à la Vie dévote*;[10] and *De l'Art de regner* (1665). In my opinion, Le Moyne's most notable successes in verse, those works which most deserve a twentieth-century reading, are the following: *Hymnes de la Sagesse divine, et de l'Amour divin* (1639 and 1641); the verse portraits of Lais, Actaeon, Hannibal, Andromeda, and Semiramis included in *Les Peintures morales*; his epic, *Saint Louis, ou la Sainte Couronne reconquise* (1658); and *Entretiens et Lettres poëtiques* (1665).

Le Moyne cultivated the martial, encomiastic vein early in his career. To celebrate the feats of Louis XIII he wrote a nonextant ballet produced for the Jesuit College of Reims (1628) and a series of odes in the style of Malherbe: "Les Triomphes de Louys le Juste" (1629; renamed "Hydre deffaite," 1650) and a 600-line "Portrait du Roy passant les Alpes" (1629; renamed "Les Alpes humiliées," 1650). These poems, martial in theme, are not epics. However, by 1641 Le Moyne conceived a project for a heroic poem on the subject of King Louis IX's Egyptian Crusade. And from 1650 on he dwelt in the professed House of the Jesuit Order, rue Saint-Antoine, on the Ile-Saint-Louis. The newly constructed house and church were dedicated to Saint Louis. Over the façade was placed a statue of Louis IX beneath the arms of France; inside were paintings by Simon Vouet, one celebrating Saint Louis' apotheosis, another depicting King Louis XIII as he offers the plans of the church to his ancestor in heaven. It was in this atmosphere that Father Le Moyne worked away on his nationalistic, dynastic, and religious poem. Although a first draft of seven books, containing some 7,200 lines, was published in 1653, Le Moyne revised this fragment extensively, transforming the un-

---

[10] Pascal ridicules Le Moyne in the *Provinciales* 9: "Et c'est en quoy le P. le Moyne a acquis beaucoup de reputation par le livre de *la Devotion aisée*, qu'il a fait à ce dessein. C'est là qu'il fait une peinture tout à fait charmante de la devotion. Jamais personne ne l'a connuë comme luy. [. . .] Mon Reverend Pere, je vous assure que, si vous ne m'aviez dit que le P. le Moyne est l'Autheur de cette peinture, j'aurois dit que c'eust esté quelque impie qui l'auroit faite à dessein de tourner les Saints en ridicule"; and 11: "Direz-vous que la maniere si profane et si coquette dont vostre P. le Moyne a parlé de la pieté dans sa *Devotion aisée* soit plus propre à donner du respect que du mépris pour l'idée qu'il forme de la vertu chrestienne? Tout son livre des *Peintures Morales* respire-t-il autre chose et dans sa prose et dans ses vers, qu'un esprit plein de la vanité et des folies du monde?"

derlying themes, the plot, and the style, before he gave to the world the final version of eighteen books and 17,880 lines in 1658.[11]

---

[11] For a discussion of the heroic vein in Le Moyne's work as a whole, Gross-Kiefer, *Le Dynamisme cosmique*, pp. 52-61, and Ulriksen, "Pierre Le Moyne—poète baroque français," pp. 32-33; for seventeenth-century notions of heroism and nobility, including Le Moyne's, F.E. Sutcliffe, *Guez de Balzac et son temps: Littérature et politique* (Paris, 1959), chap. 3.

# 3  *"Saint Louis": A Plot Résumé*

Given the lack of modern editions, here follows a rather detailed résumé of the plot.

BOOK 1.   The Christian army is based at Damietta. In Cairo, the Sultan Mélédin plots against Saint Louis. Mélédor, a suitor for the hand of Mélédin's daughter, Zahide, offers to negotiate with the crusaders and, when ushered into the royal presence, to assassinate Louis. The negotiations do take place. Although the vision of an angel dissuades Mélédor from his violent scheme, the old Saracen ambassador Garaman presents King Louis with the gift of a poisoned suit of armor. The messengers then dine and are lodged for the night in a magnificent tent on the walls of which are tapestried Louis' early exploits in war.

BOOK 2.   Béthunes arrives from Acre with news of Alphonse de Poitiers, whose contingent was separated from Louis' by a storm when they both were crossing the Mediterranean Sea. Béthunes tells how, having capsized on the coast of Palestine, Poitiers saved the lives of certain princes of the local crusader states: a widow, Lisamante, who was attacked by a panther, and a married couple, Raymond and Belinde, threatened by pirates. Lisamante and Raymond of course recounted to Poitiers their highly romantic past histories. Béthunes' story terminated, Poitiers arrives with his troops, accompanied by Lisamante, Raymond, and Belinde. After dinner Coucy recounts to the newcomers what happened to the main army in their absence: specifically, how the fleet suffered from the tempest and then victoriously resisted a savage onslaught from the Saracen navy, led by the intrepid Forcadin.

BOOK 3.   Coucy continues his tale. The Christians landed successfully near Damietta, vanquishing the Saracen army sent to hold the beaches. The next morning they were informed by Léonin, a Christian from Damietta, how his beloved, Alcinde, slaughtered a crocodile, the tutelary deity of the town: as a result of this act, the frenzied Egyptians massacred the native Christian population, burned the town, and abandoned it to the crusaders—but not before executing Alcinde. Coucy concludes by describing the triumphant entry of the French host into Damietta in the guise of a corpus Christi procession.

Book 4.   A magnificent tourney is held in the Christian camp. Toward the end of the day's activities, an unknown knight, a giant, comes from without to challenge the crusaders. After defeating six of their best knights, the "Assassin" challenges King Louis and employs a genuine war lance against him, but is defeated.

Book 5.   Le Moyne describes the various contingents of the French army as it leaves Damietta in the direction of Cairo: this is the marshalling of the troops. Meanwhile, Mélédin's aged counsellor, the sorcerer Mirème, offers to invoke phantoms from hell, in aid of the Saracen cause. Inside one of the great pyramids the shade of Saladin instructs Mélédin that the Christians shall be repulsed only if the Sultan sacrifices the life of his own son or daughter.

Book 6.   Mélédin prepares to sacrifice his daughter Zahide on an old Pagan altar located on the banks of the Nile. The young prince Muratan offers to die in his sister's place and, when Mélédin refuses, stabs himself. Zahide rushes to Muratan's assistance; in the confusion, brother and sister both fall into the river. Zahide is fished out of the water alive by Almasonte, a warrior-maiden from Syria. Meanwhile, the Nile floods, and the Christian army retreats with dignity to a hill on which lie the ruins of a castle Joseph built in the days of Exodus.

Book 7.   A great Saracen host arrives, transported on the Nile in boats. This gives Le Moyne an occasion to list the Moslem contingents. A pitched battle takes place. Despite feats of valor by Forcadin, the Saracens are repulsed, and King Louis himself slays the redoubtable Olgan, who was responsible for the death of Alcinde in Damietta.

Book 8.   At night King Louis prays to heaven, and his prayer is answered. Saint Michael informs him that his tears have dammed the flood. Michael takes Louis to heaven on a throne of fire. There Louis observes the various orders of the blessed, speaks to his late father, King Louis VIII, and beholds Christ in majesty. Christ offers Louis a choice between the crown of Rome, the crown of Byzantium, and Christ's own crown of thorns. Louis chooses the latter and places it on his head. Christ then informs Louis of his future trials in life and of his royal descendants, the Kings of France down to Louis XIII.

BOOK 9.   On the return voyage to earth, Michael instructs King Louis on the topography and on the past and future history of the planet. The waters of the Nile recede. The Saracens withdraw, and the crusaders bury their dead and proceed on toward Cairo. Meanwhile, on the Nile Almasonte's warship engages in combat with a vessel commanded by Louis' nephew, Archambaut de Bourbon. This encounter is rendered tragic by the fact that Almasonte saved Bourbon's life previously in Syria and that she has fallen in love with him. Bourbon performs feats of exceptional valor and defeats the enemy captain, discovering only after the adversary's cask is removed that he has apparently killed his benefactress. Almasonte is restored to life, however, and she and Zahide become Bourbon's prisoners.

BOOK 10.   Blocked by the Nile, the French army seeks to build a bridge over the waters. However, a hostile dragon prevents workmen from cutting down trees in his forest. King Louis prepares to do battle with the dragon and, for this purpose, dons the poisoned armor given to him by the Saracens in Book 1. Lightning from heaven burns away the armor, while sparing Louis' body. To interpret the symbolic import of these marvels, prelates are sent to consult a solitary hermitess, Alégonde, widow of the crusader Aymon de Bourbon and, therefore, related to Archambaut de Bourbon. She declares that only a Bourbon shall be permitted to overcome the dragon, and recounts hers and her husband's life-stories.

BOOK 11.   Bourbon visits Alégonde. She tells him of his noble descendants, including Henry IV, Louis XIII, and Louis XIV. She also urges him to conquer his growing love for Almasonte. Bourbon returns to the camp, and, after a vision from heaven, he renounces Almasonte and releases her and Zahide from captivity. Almasonte is furious. Meanwhile, Mélédor (cf. Book 1) and a certain Alzir sneak by night into the Christian camp in order to deliver their beloveds, Zahide and Almasonte, respectively. Having killed sentries and stolen the armor of Bourbon and his page, they then unwittingly duel the two casked Saracen maidens. Zahide kills her suitor Mélédor; Alzir slays Almasonte, then commits suicide.

Book 12.   Having donned the armor of his ancestor, Aymon de Bourbon, young Archambaut de Bourbon fells the dragon. The French army cuts down the forest and builds a fortified bridge over the Nile. A Saracen host comes to attack them, supported by a contingent of elephants. Louis shoots an arrow into the eye of one elephant, thereby causing a stampede, and the Saracens are repulsed. Then Forcadin and Zahide lead a surprise night sortie into the Christian camp. They are repulsed by Louis but not before having taken Lisamante prisoner.

Book 13.   The old Sultan Mélédin lusts for Lisamante, who craftily agrees to become his bride. On their wedding night, urged on by the biblical Judith, come from heaven to sustain her, Lisamante slays the drunken Mélédin. Lisamante and Judith then miraculously walk across the Nile, where the Syrian princess is welcomed by Béthunes, who has fallen in love with her. In the Saracen camp Mélédin is buried, Forcadin elected generalissimo, and native Egyptian Christians massacred. Mirème invokes a host of fire-demons who form a battery and, with the assistance of Mirème's own, man-made Greek fire, burn down the fortified bridge and would have annihilated the crusaders altogether, had God not put an end to the assault.

Book 14.   Unable to cross the Nile, Louis prays to God for succor. The divinity sends an angel who opens a land passage across the river. The Christian army crosses to the other side, where Robert d'Artois particularly distinguishes himself in the ensuing combat. Artois penetrates inside the walls of Mansourah and slays Drogasse, the governor of the place, before he in turn falls and is martyred for the faith.

Book 15.   The battle continues. Lisamante duels Zahide. When Zahide is wounded by a poisoned arrow shot by one of her own suitors, Alfasel, who hoped to fell Lisamante, Zahide is taken prisoner and Alfasel commits suicide. Louis and Bourbon overcome Forcadin's troops but then must endure an assault from twenty elephants. Coucy perishes. Raymond and Belinde slay one of the elephants which, in falling, takes the life of Belinde. Louis wounds two elephants, thus stemming the tide, and remains master of the field, but is himself wounded by a poisoned arrow.

BOOK 16.   Funeral honors are extended to the fallen Belinde; Raymond expires from chagrin over her corpse. Meanwhile, King Louis and Zahide languish from their wounds. In a subterranean hall, Mirème invokes demons, upon which Mélédin's ghost informs him that Louis can only be cured by water from the Matariya Fountain, a holy place where the Virgin Mary washed the infant Jesus' swaddling-clothes during the Flight into Egypt. Mirème surrounds the fountain with enchantments. On the Christian side Brenne, who has fallen in love with Zahide, and Bourbon set out to fetch water from the holy fountain. Bourbon performs feats of valor and overcomes the demonic obstacles in his path, finally slaying a monster, who turns out to be Mirème himself in Satanic guise.

BOOK 17.   Bourbon and Brenne return to camp with the holy water. Louis and Zahide are miraculously restored to health, and no less miraculously Zahide perceives a vision of Mary. So Zahide converts to Christianity, is baptized, and engaged to Brenne. A casked Saracen appears to challenge the French army for Zahide. Brenne gives combat to the Saracen. At the last minute the enemy's cask is severed, and Zahide rushes in to save her brother Muratan, who survived his attempted suicide in the Nile. Muratan also converts to the true faith, and the crusaders prepare to attack the Saracen camp.

BOOK 18.   The two hosts face each other for the final battle. Forcadin slays Lisamante and Béthunes, who sought to protect her by interposing his own body against Forcadin's blows. Louis fells several redoubtable adversaries and, at last, Forcadin himself. Proceeding to Mélédin's tent, Louis slays a final adversary but is presented with two crowns of thorns. One is authentic, the other an enchantment by Mirème which can infect the entire crusader army with the plague. But as a result of Louis' prayers, a ray from heaven burns the false crown, and the true one places itself on the king's saintly brow.

## 4  *Two Problems: Historical Inaccuracy and Slavish Imitation*

Before proceeding farther, I wish to consider two objections that have been made to Le Moyne's epic by scholars. One concerns the fact that, more than Tasso and Camoens, more than his contemporary Chapelain, Le Moyne contradicts history.[12] Historically, King Louis IX of France seized Damietta in 1249 but then was defeated and taken prisoner at the battle of Mansourah in February 1250. Ransomed at great cost, Louis returned to France, his crusade a monumental defeat. As far as we can tell from a prediction of future events in heaven, in the 1653 version Le Moyne intended *grosso modo* to follow the true story. However, by 1658, *Saint Louis, ou le Heros chrestien* became *Saint Louis, ou la Sainte Couronne reconquise*. Christ's crown of thorns now is the central image of the poem; Louis undertakes the crusade not to convert Saracens or to free the Holy Land but uniquely in order to seize the relic; and the poem ends with his doing so, after a complete victory over the enemy. Obviously sensitive to criticism on this point, in his *Dissertation du poëme heroïque* Le Moyne postulates some misfortune in the lives of all heroes, for example, Hercules, Regulus, Samson, David, and the Macchabees.[13] He also justifies an "epical" happy ending for a "partial action" even when the

---

[12] For this problem, consult Chérot, *Étude sur la vie et les œuvres*, chaps. 10 and 11; Edelman, *Attitudes of Seventeenth-Century France*, chap. 5; and Maskell, *The Historical Epic*, chap. 9.

[13] "Que l'on me nomme un Heros de reputation, qui n'ait jamais esté malheureux: qui n'ait rien souffert en sa vie ou à sa mort. [. . .] Disons donc qu'il est ordinaire aux Heros d'estre malheureux: Disons encore davantage, et nous dirons la verité; sans estre bien malheureux, on ne peut estre qu'un Heros fort mediocre." *Dissertation* [p. iv], printed in *Les Œuvres poétiques* without numbered pagination. This *Dissertation*, dating from 1666, differs slightly from the *Traité du poëme heroïque* of 1658.

protagonist's life ends unhappily (as in the careers of Achilles and Aeneas).[14] Finally, he claims, with more than a little Jesuitical casuistry, that the plot of an epic must be historically accurate, or generally believed to be so;[15] therefore, his *Saint Louis* is grounded in history and "tradition" (e.g., legend) and its action is more or less true, for in both history and his epic Louis goes to Egypt, wins battles, brings back relics, and acquires the Crown of Thorns. Unfortunately for Le Moyne's thesis, however, the crown of thorns was not one of the relics the historical Louis brought back from Egypt; in 1238, some ten years before the Crusade, he purchased it from the Venetians who had acquired it from Baudouin II, the Frankish Emperor of Byzantium. And Le Moyne gives the impression that the Egyptian campaign, including the Battle of Mansourah, can be thought of as a series of unalloyed victories, whereas such was most certainly not the case. What the poet in fact did was to set his hero a fictional task and use history to buttress his fictional account of it; whenever history conflicted with the poetic structure, it was simply rejected.

In Le Moyne's defense, it can be said that his public was less meticulous in such matters than modern historians of literature. Indeed, throughout the seventeenth century Louis IX was celebrated as a great warrior and victorious crusader.[16] It is also probable that our twentieth-century public is not much better informed

---

[14] *Dissertation* [pp. viii and ix]: "Ce n'est pas assez que l'Action soit loüable, il faut de plus qu'elle soit heureuse. La dignité du Heros, et l'edification du Public demande cela: et il importe extrémement, que l'issuë en soit la plus specieuse, et la plus éclatante qu'il se pourra; afin qu'elle pique le cœur des Grands: et que l'emulation les porte à de pareilles entreprises, par le desir, et par l'esperance d'un pareil succés.

[. . .] On en demanderoit trop, si l'on en demandoit davantage à mon Heros. Achille, Ulysse, Enée, Godefroy, n'ont pas tant cousté à faire: et leurs Actions, à beaucoup moins que cela, ont passé pour illustres, et pour heroïques. Il n'importe que la Guerre ne luy ait pas esté si heureuse en toutes choses: ces malheurs n'entrent point dans mon Sujet: ils sont posterieurs à l'Action sur laquelle j'ay travaillé: ils n'en corrompent point le succés: et pourveu que la fin où je la conduis soit heureuse, tout ce qui vient aprés cette heureuse fin estant hors de ma besogne, et n'appartenant point à l'Action, ni à la Fable fondée sur l'Action, il n'y a point de loy qui m'oblige à le garantir: et l'on me tiendroit une rigueur sans exemple, si l'on m'en vouloit faire comptable."

[15] *Dissertation* [p. iv] and *Dichtungslehren der Romania*, p. 460: "Il faut que l'Action soit vraye ou tenuë pour vraye, sur la foy de la Tradition ou de l'Histoire. [. . .] Le premier soin du Poëte sera de bastir sur un fonds ferme et solide; sur une verité prise de l'Histoire, ou receuë de la Tradition."

[16] Edelman, *Attitudes of Seventeenth-Century France.*

on early French history than Mlle de Scudéry's, nor does the modern reader judge an epic or a historical novel on the basis of its fidelity to what historians tell us the past really was like. Did not the medieval *trouvères* transform Carolingian and early British history far more than Le Moyne—and have not their "myths" of Roland and Oliver, of Tristan and Isolt, of Lancelot, Guinevere, and King Arthur become History for most people in our society? Do we condemn Schiller's *Die Jungfrau von Orleans* because in that play Joan of Arc is killed on the field of battle? Do we condemn Anouilh because he bases the action of *Becket ou l'Honneur de Dieu* on a conflict between the Anglo-Saxon archbishop and the Norman king, whereas, in reality, Becket was as Norman-French in language, culture, and origins as King Henry? I submit that Le Moyne's ceremonial, baroque representation of the thirteenth century and Anouilh's witty, sarcastic one of the twelfth century do not necessarily distort the reality of those times more than does the simplistic Age of Faith conceived by some moderns. But, in my opinion, the key to the problem is this: the creative writer, whether he be Chrétien de Troyes, Pierre Le Moyne, or Jean Anouilh, has a right to transform history as he chooses. Literature is not history and must follow its own laws. The rules of epic in the seventeenth century and the particular mode of ceremonial heroic romance in which Tasso and Le Moyne chose to write required a happy ending. And Le Moyne himself, a man who in other contexts esteemed himself to be a historian, proclaims in the *Dissertation* the poet's freedom with regard to history.[17] Le Moyne merely exercised that freedom given to all artists; it is his privilege to write a heroic romance instead of a chronicle, to transform history into art.

Some people have claimed that Le Moyne lacks originality, that, like his contemporaries Scudéry, Chapelain, and Desmarets, he follows the rules too closely. It is true that *Saint Louis* contains an enormous number of conventions, themes, and motifs, all of which are derived from Homer, Virgil, Lucan, Ronsard, and

---

[17] *Dissertation* [p. v]: "Et puis, le Critique ignoreroit-il, que le Parnasse est un Païs libre?" Le Moyne follows Aristotle and Ronsard in preferring poetry to history and credibility to truth. He claims that the *Vraisemblable* represents a synthesis of history and legend, and that it is esthetically more *rare* and *ingénieux* to combine the true and the false than to limit oneself only to the true.

Tasso. In his approach to the problem of genre, Le Moyne is less spontaneous than d'Aubigné and Saint-Amant; *Saint Louis* is a neo-classical epic pure and simple, its narrative structure based entirely upon classical and Italian models. Although Le Moyne speaks greatly of Virgil, he owes the most to Tasso, to *la Gerusalemme liberata* and *la Gerusalemme conquistata*.[18] In Tasso, as in Le Moyne, Christians undertake a victorious crusade against Saracens. An older hero in command (Goffredo, Louis IX) is assisted by a vigorous young warrior (Rinaldo, Bourbon); from both men will descend a glorious line. Rinaldo-Bourbon loves but gives up a Saracen princess (Armida, Almasonte) and dispells enchantments over a forest where the crusaders were cutting trees. A holy person in solitude (Il mago d'Ascalona, Alégonde) explains that Rinaldo-Bourbon is destined to deliver the forest and why. On the other side stand an indomitable old man (Aladino, Mélédin), an indomitable, fierce, younger warrior (Argante or Solimano, Forcadin), and a wily old sorcerer (Ismeno, Mirème), all of whom perish in the end. Before this, however, Aladino-Mélédin plots to massacre the Christian minority inhabiting his city. The Saracens indulge in a night sortie; later, Goffredo-Louis is wounded by an arrow. And demons attack the Franks, who are defended by angels. The action is complicated by the exploits of a husband and wife team (Odoardo and Gildippe, Raymond and Belinde) and of warrior maidens, one of whom was born in romantic circumstances and suckled by a tigress (Clorinda, Lisamante), and one of whom is mistakenly killed in battle by a lover or suitor (Clorinda, Almasonte). A Saracen *bellatrix* is captured, converted, and married (Armida, Zahide). And a husband and wife or two lovers or a brother and sister are (almost) martyred, each seeking to give his life for the other (Olindo and Sofronia, Zahide and Muratan or Alcinde and Léonin).

I shall simply point out that Le Moyne was not the only writer of his age to pastiche Tasso. *Alaric, Clovis*, and *La Pucelle*, not to speak of a host of Italian and Spanish epics, including a *Jerusalén conquistada* (1609) by Lope de Vega, all follow in the traces of the divine

---

[18] See Chandler B. Beall, *La Fortune du Tasse en France* (Eugene, 1942); Joseph Cottaz, *L'Influence des théories du Tasse sur l'épopée en France* (Paris, 1942); Joyce G. Simpson, *Le Tasse et la littérature et l'art baroques en France* (Paris, 1962).

Torquato. And they are neither more nor less original than Renaissance sonneteers (including Du Bellay, Ronsard, Garcilaso de la Vega, Herrera, Sidney, Spenser, and Shakespeare) who wrote in the wake of Petrarch, or the flood of late *chansons de geste* (including such masterpieces as *Renaud de Montauban*, *Garin le Lorrain*, and *Aspremont*), all based on earlier texts, made up, as it were, of clichés from previous epics. We do not automatically assume Boccaccio to be superior to Chaucer, or Chrétien de Troyes superior to Wolfram von Eschenbach merely because Chrétien and Boccaccio came first. Up until fairly recent times the composition of all Western poetry was based on a tradition of *imitatio*. The notion of strictly original creation is modern. It is a Romantic or post-Romantic myth, and in the course of world literature this myth proves to be an exception, indeed an aberration.

# 5   *Themes and Motifs in a Baroque Epic*

Among the strongest impressions the reader receives from *Saint Louis* is one of splendor and magnificence. "La valeur est pompeuse, et la pompe est vaillante" (Book 18, p. 224 A) says Le Moyne of the Christian host before its ultimate ordeal. Grandiose speeches and battle scenes serve as backdrops to a martial saint-king whose every word and deed are solemn, heroic, and hierarchical. The faith of the crusaders is embodied in ceremonial and liturgy, in color and pageantry. The technical skill of the duels, the ostentatious rhetoric of speeches, the spectacle of religious events— funeral, baptism, marriage, corpus Christi procession—fulfill the demands of an age. Le Moyne caters to, and recreates in his epic, the decorum and *solemne* of courtly civility. His poem celebrates the external forms of grandiose living, for in his world reality manifests itself immediately in appearance. Like the plays of Rotrou, Mairet, Tristan, Du Ryer, and, above all, Corneille, it proclaims a glorious chivalric-Christian ideal that has perhaps never existed but in men's minds. Indeed, in contrast to Tasso, whose characters, greater than life, often appear downcast and alone, Le Moyne's people (at least the Franks) work together for the common good, in harmony, contributing to social order.

Perhaps the most striking festivity recounted in the epic is a tournament (Book 4), which corresponds, *mutatis mutandis*, to the "games" of the *Iliad* and the *Aeneid* and to the courtly festivities of medieval romance. However, as the four contingents march onto the field, each clad in special colors and proclaiming allegiance to a particular form of love, with a page singing or declaiming a cartel, we realize that Pierre Le Moyne's carrousel does not correspond to the reality of a thirteenth-century tourney. The historical Louis IX never witnessed a gigantic artificial rock that opens to display a grotto inside, or an elephant with a globe on its back that also opens before our eyes. Le Moyne's tourney is fully in the spirit of his own age. Of the two most famous comparable spectacles in the seventeenth century, one celebrated the double royal wedding of Louis XIII and his sister to the Infantes of Spain (1612); the other, *Les Plaisirs de l'Isle enchantée*, fêted Louis XIV's love for Mlle de La Vallière (1664). These tourneys continued the medieval tradition of martial games (tilting at a ring, tilting at the quintain, or real jousting) but also gave rise to pageantry and spectacular displays of luxury in clothing, armor, and pavilions, to sparkle and a riot of colors. The carrousel itself included an elaborate entry of the troops, with special attention accorded to the leader, his heralds, and their pages. Le Moyne's elephant and the fireworks "invented" by Coucy are taken directly from the royal carrousel of 1612. It is surely not coincidental that another Jesuit, Claude-François Menestrier, author of a *Traité des tournois, joustes, carrousels, et autres spectacles publics* (1669), was the leading expert in this matter as well as in funeral ceremonies (cf. his treatise, *Des Decorations funebres où il est amplement traité des Tentures, des Lumières, des Mausolées, Catafalques, Inscriptions et autres Ornemens funebres*, 1684), or that, for the seventeenth-century public, the tourney, with its martial aura and cartels on old romance subjects, was presumed to be a peculiarly traditional, medieval institution.[19]

In an age in which the topic *mundus theatrum* was in its greatest vogue, exploited by writers as varied as Ronsard, Shakespeare, Marvell, Calderón, Gracián, Corneille, Rotrou, and d'Aubigné, it is not surprising that Pierre Le Moyne should have written a long didactic poem entitled "Le Theatre du sage." Similarly, in his epic the tourney takes place as if in a gigantic theatre, with King Louis and the old knights as spectators; Zahide is sacrificed on an altar dating from Pagan times, constructed in the form of a theatre (Book 6); Saracens arrive on boats to attack the Franks, as if they were participating in a Roman circus, providing a theatrical spectacle for their adversaries (Book 7); and God, his angels, and Saint Louis look down from heaven on a world-stage where glory and

---

[19] See Edelman, *Attitudes of Seventeenth-Century France*, chap. 3.

ambition seek to dominate the scene but end in the grave:

> Cette boule flotante et demi-submergée,
> De son poids soustenuë, et de son poids plongée,
> Est l'espace, dit-il, où le mortel orgueil,
> Croit avoir un Theatre, et n'a qu'un vain cercueil.
> [. . .] Sur ce Point cependant les Passions humaines,
> Font leurs tragiques Jeux, ont leurs sanglantes Scenes.
>
> (Book 9: p. 101B)

The play, like the tournament, stands somewhere on the frontier between the sacred and the profane. Its gratuitous, ludic quality softens the reality of warfare, interposing distance and decorum between the public and the events recounted. The "reality" of the plot is in the author's mind. The public is expected to accept it, however absurd it may appear, for he presents us with art, that is, artifice, not life. It is equally true, however, that beleaguered Christians and the heavenly-borne King Louis do participate in the action—they become players on the world stage. As actors, not mere spectators, they are involved in the drama, a different kind of performance, one of God's making, on a different level altogether.

If life is a play, and the theatre an image for the world, life is based upon play, that is, wit and jest, and its reality embodied in artistic illusion. The Nile flood (Books 6 and 7) gives rise to some extraordinary effects of illusion through metamorphosis, and of paradox through illusion. Thus, at night, the waters rise in the darkness, and one cannot distinguish between land and river. With the coming of dawn, however, before our eyes a floating desert comes into view, with fishes and boats in place of plowmen; the crusaders are astonished by this desert of water, a floating tomb where trees have drowned and boats cut into the land like plows. Earlier in the story, when the crusaders left Cyprus for Egypt, their fleet appeared to be a forest floating in the air or an armed camp rolling on the seas.

> Jamais un Camp plus beau ne roula sur la Mer;
> Ni plus belles forests ne volerent en l'Air.

> L'Aurore à son lever en parut étonnée;
> Le Soleil pour la voir avança la journée;
> Et semble de rayons plus clairs et mieux dorez,
> Vouloir peindre les Lys sur nos masts arborez.

(Book 2: p. 21B)

This is the same *verkehrte Welt* flood-motif to be found in much baroque literature, as well as in classical Antiquity and the Middle Ages,[20] but Le Moyne develops it in greater detail than others do. In this upside-down world, nature has lost her proper function, and the unnatural triumphs over the natural. Confusion and disorder reign. Yet, for Le Moyne, *impossibilia*, even if of demonic origin, make a fascinating spectacle. And in several *Peintures morales* ("Laïs," "Andromede," "Acteon"), he celebrates horrible, monstrous, yet electrifying myths of metamorphosis.

As can be observed from my last quote, a comparable phenomenon occurs in pathetic fallacy, with aspects of Nature participating in the lives of men. When the corpus Christi is rolled into Damietta, the sun withdraws and palm trees bow down (Book 3). Lisamante walks on the Nile; therefore, the moon stops her course in astonishment, and stars come closer to light her way (Book 13). Saint Louis or Belinde dying, stars, flags, and banners beam less brightly, rubies, gold, and torches go pale; Saint Louis cured, tents, flags, trumpets, equipment, and armor shine and sound with joy (Books 16 and 17). On one occasion, a scimitar, fearing to kill a Christian maiden, bends away from her (Book 3). Like his fellow epic poets, Pierre Le Moyne relishes verbal play on the theme of violent death. A host of warriors perish "appropriately," according to their state in life or dominant trait. Thus, a Greek musician is pierced through the ears, a swimmer's arms are cut off, a singer's vocal chord is severed, a fencer dies, his arms outstretched, fencing with the sea. And, in an extraordinary scene, after having shot his mistress Zahide in the neck by mistake

---

[20] Ernst Robert Curtius, *Europäische Literatur und lateinisches Mittelalter* (Berne, 1948), chap. 1. Also consult Rousset, *La Littérature de l'âge baroque*, chaps. 1 and 6; Erik Michaëlsson, "L'eau, centre de métaphores et de métamorphoses dans la littérature française de la première moitié du XVIIe siècle: Le miroir de l'eau et le déluge," *Orbis Litterarum*, 14 (1959), 121-173; Gilbert Delley, *L'Assomption de la Nature dans la lyrique française de l'Age baroque* (Berne, 1969), pp. 260-309; Jean-Pierre Chauveau, "La mer et l'imagination des poètes au XVIIe siècle," *XVIIe Siècle*, Nos. 86-87 (1970), 107-134.

with an arrow (Book 15), Alfasel commits suicide, strangling himself in the neck with his own bow-string, so that his heart, which ever loved her, will remain intact even in death. He cries out to Zahide:

> [. . .] Je le tiens [,] luy dit-il, je le tiens et l'ameine,
> Le barbare Meurtrier, dont la main inhumaine,
> D'une erreur sacrilege a violé ce corps,
> Aux Graces consacré, comblé de leurs tresors.
> Prononcez son arrest, decernez son supplice,
> Les bras auteurs du crime, en feront la justice.
> Vostre bouche se taist: mais vos yeux offensez,
> De leur regards mourans me comdamnent assez.
> La voix de vostre sang se fait assez entendre;
> Je ne puis la dedire, et ne m'en puis défendre.
> Au moins, illustre sang, moderèz vostre voix,
> Je sçay ce qu'elle veut, et ce que je luy dois.
> Quoy que vous demandiez, soit mon cœur, ou ma teste,
> A tout executer ma main est toute preste.
> Mais pourray-je sans crime, attenter sur un cœur,
> Que l'Amour vous soûmit, dés qu'il en fut vainqueur?
> Qu'il reste donc entier, comme il reste fidelle,
> Que vostre image y soit, s'il se peut, immortelle:
> Et que le premier feu dont il fut allumé,
> Avecque mon Esprit y demeure enfermé.
>
> (Book 15: p. 188A & B)

Whenever the Saracens take the field, Frenchmen are offered a spectacle of exotic banners, accoutrements, and musical instruments, of vast foreign hosts who "Mesloient l'affreux au riche, et la pompe d'horreur" (Book 18: p. 244B). In contrast, on the march the crusaders are compared to a Virgilian bee-hive (Book 5). That is, their monarch, Louis IX, through speech, action, and his mere presence, controls the host, ranging it within the bounds of order. A figure of *sapientia* as well as of *fortitudo*, he raises the spirits of his men. He is at the center of his host, the troops marshalled around him under his command. His is the image of the obedient, impassible, serene Christian monarch, who, like Goffredo in the *Conquistata*, never hesitates and never doubts. This is counter-reformation militancy in its strongest form.

Le Moyne's narrative structure adheres to the same sense of hierarchy and order. His story begins with the capture of Damietta and proceeds to recount the complete triumph of Louis in Egypt.[21] Of course, he is not afraid to digress, for his is a pre-Racinian notion of composition, in which juxtaposition of disparate styles and a multiple story-line are not to be condemned. These digressions usually take the form of "episodes," what in the novel were to be called *tiroirs*, that is, stories told by one character, a delegated narrator, to others in the course of the poem. Imitating the *Odyssey* and the *Aeneid*, Le Moyne begins his epic *in medias res*, not *ab ovo*. And Homer, Virgil, Ariosto, and Tasso all give sufficient precedent for Le Moyne to indulge in retelling past events and predicting future ones, as well as other increments that do not forward the plot line: a tournament, the marshalling of troops on both sides, and a voyage to heaven where the hero receives useful instruction. It is to be noted that, like Ariosto, Le Moyne does not mind piling up digressions early in the narrative. With the exception of Muratan's story (Book 17), all of them occur in the first eleven books, with only Books 6 and 7 devoted entirely to narrative. Indeed, Le Moyne's propensity in this direction increased from 1653 to 1658, for comparing his two versions of the epic, we discover that the seven books of *Le Heros chrestien* have been expanded into almost nine books in *La Sainte Couronne reconquise*, due to the addition of the tournament and the story of Lisamante's childhood; and that the exciting scene when Mirème evokes demons and the subsequent sacrifice of Zahide have been moved from Book 2 (in 1653) to Books 5 and 6 (in 1658). In fact, in the final version of *Saint Louis* the war itself properly speaking does not begin until Book 7. Pierre Le Moyne is less interested in drama than in celebration. His digressions are as important as the main action, and he expects us to savor them. He proceeds slowly with the narrative, his complex story line treated as a work of art in itself, a thing of beauty guaranteed to stimulate *meraviglia* in those who partake of it.

---

[21] In the *Dissertation* Le Moyne insists upon the importance of a coherent, unified structure in epic and assures us that *Saint Louis* leaves nothing to be desired in this respect [pp. vi, xii-xiv], and *Dichtungslehren der Romania*, pp. 462-464.

## 6   *The Ethics of Heroism*

Ethically, *Saint Louis* resembles that other great crusade epic, *La Chanson de Roland*. Although Le Moyne has no sense whatsoever of class-struggle or of the intra-cultural tensions that render the political context of the *Roland* so problematic, he and Turold share one fundamental postulate: that *Paien unt tort e Chrestien unt dreit* (1015). It is only after having recognized and accepted this basis of Le Moyne's universe that we can come to grips with the more striking manifestations of "Christian injustice" in this Christian melodrama. For example, in Book 3 Alcinde, a female Christian inhabitant of Damietta, "émeuë et de zele et de foy" (p. 33B), willfully and without warning kills a crocodile, the tutelary deity of her city; the Saracens then slaughter 200 Christians in retaliation, including the murderess. In Book 13, although Lisamante, a prisoner of the Saracens, yields to the Sultan's proposal of marriage, on their wedding night she murders the bridegroom in his drunken slumber, upon which the Saracens execute still more Christians. A modern reader might well excuse the Moslem retaliations and condemn Alcinde and Lisamante both for fanaticism and an absence of fair-play. Yet it is clear that Le Moyne sides one hundred percent with his *femmes fortes*. According to his crusading Jesuit ethos, a Christian can do no wrong. He is always correct, those who oppose him in error. Although both Alcinde and Lisamante commit acts repugnant to society's commonly accepted standards, the notion of ethics, as we moderns know it, is transformed. Rather than that a Christian hero be considered good because he conforms to given standards, his actions are proved good simply because he is the man who commits them. In other words, right and wrong are determined not with reference to a pre-established moral code but by the hero himself, who has a particular end in view, and the means always justify the end.

A second point is that, although conflict may appear to exist, it is illusory. God's free gift of grace is ever available to his servants. Le Moyne's universe has no place for tragedy. Under God's eternally vigilant eye, the world is good (cf. *Hymnes, et Eloges poetiques*, including "La Sagesse divine" and "L'Amour divin"). When a hero dies (as do Robert d'Artois, Coucy, Belinde, Raymond, Lisamante, and Béthunes), we know for certain that they proceed directly to their respective thrones in heaven. However, as Louis informs his army in more than one speech, the crusaders can also count on victory. The Lord of Hosts who performed miracles in the past—who made the Flood recede, destroyed Sodom and Gomorrah, helped David vanquish Goliath, and preserved Joseph and Moses from the wrath of Pharaoh—shall succor his Chosen People of the New Covenant. And so he does. God continually intervenes in the world. Through intermediaries— guardian angels or Saint Michael, or from God's own fire and thunder, miracle after miracle occurs, sparing individual heroes and the army as a whole. The Nile in rage, demons from hell, monstrous dragons, Saracen armies are impotent against the will of God.

Le Moyne's characters do not grow, do not develop in the course of the narrative. In contrast to Tasso's, his people display little or no weakness, withdrawing neither from the battlefield nor from their Christian duty. Bourbon is much less impulsive than Rinaldo and Tancredi; although Brenne loves Zahide passionately, their amours are irrelevant to the plot-line until after she becomes Lisamante's prisoner and is about to convert. Indeed, the only change a Zahide, a Muratan, or a Bourbon undergoes is sudden conversion, brought about by divine miracle, whereas Louis himself and the majority of his men are ever steadfast in their devotion to the Cause. Driven by *ardeur* or *vertu*, they commit acts beyond the ordinary in a mood of enthusiasm and ecstasy. No hesitation, no waiting, separate an impulse from the act it gives rise to. The idea comes first, the character second, determined by the idea. What he says he does and is. Furthermore, this kind of hero does not become great but is slowly and surely recognized to be so. And he commits great deeds because he is born to commit them. His virtues are present from the beginning, are part of him, since he is French, Christian, and the ancestor of Le Moyne's seventeenth-century patrons. As in the plays of Corneille, he inspires admiration rather than pity or terror. He is the magnanimous man par excellence, an archetype of manly virtue, a social ideal as well as an individual one. The hero does not stand alone: he is the delegate of a fictional society in the epic and the ideal of a real one in seventeenth-century France. This is not description but celebration, supreme personal splendor, and ritual play, in a truly essentialist universe.

It is true, some of Le Moyne's most splendid scenes contain speeches of will-to-power in the style of Corneille. Fortune can destroy me, cries Mélédin, but my heart and *vertu* stand firm. Since heaven will not help me, I invoke hell!

> Meledin par le sort peut estre combatu,
> Mais le sort ne sçauroit abatre sa vertu:
> Et tant que sa vertu conservera sa place,
> La Fortune à son gré, peut bien changer de face;
> Elle peut tout mesler, elle peut perdre tout;
> Le cœur de Meledin demeurera debout:
> Et c'est contre ce cœur, plus haut que mes ruïnes,
> Que le Corsaire Franc doit dresser ses machines.

(Book 1: p. 3B)

> Mene-moy si tu veux, à ces pasles demeures,
> Où le jour froid et mort n'a que d'obscures heures:
> Mets si tu veux mes yeux, à l'épreuve des fers,
> A l'épreuve des feux, qui fument aux Enfers:
> Evoque devant moy du sein des sepultures,
> Des Manes les plus noirs les terribles figures:
> Mon cœur et mon esprit intrepides par-tout,
> A tant d'objects d'horreur demeureront debout:
> Et jusqu'en ces fourneaux que la nuit environne,
> J'iray prendre de quoi m'armer pour ma Couronne.
> Si le Ciel ne m'y sert, l'Enfer m'y servira:
> Ce que le droit ne peut, le crime le pourra:
> Et le crime se change, et cesse d'estre crime,
> Quand la necessité l'a rendu legitime.

(Book 5: p. 57B)

Olgan and Forcadin scorn the enchantments Mirème has marshalled on their side; relying only on brute force, they defy both God and the world (Books 7, 13, and 18). Like Nicomède, Cléopâtre, Rodogune, Auguste, and Horace, these men apply to themselves and others the law they freely choose. Repudiating common morality, anguish, and despair, they make a decision and live up to it at any cost. Their lives are their creation. They are masters, never slaves. However, Le Moyne differs from Corneille in that these speeches are reserved to Saracens and, therefore, are not meant to be taken as models for conduct. Louis IX once indulges in a comparable tirade, proclaiming his *vertu*, but he is rebuked by God's lightning (Book 10). Zahide and Muratan convert and turn their indomitable will (which had been broken by God) to good purposes. Indeed, throughout the poem Le Moyne speaks out against man's presumption; he attacks the illusions of worldly grandeur (cf. "Le Palais de la Fortune," "Le Theatre du sage," and "De la Paix du sage") in favor of asceticism and a quite different, truly Christian grandeur.

On one occasion, Forcadin declares his independence from all contingent forces, human and divine, yet also permits Mirème to execute Christian captives, in order to appease the populace and the dead Sultan's shade:

> [Je] ne veux consulter, sur le sort des combats,
> D'autre Astre que ce fer, d'autre Dieu que ce bras,
> Tant que ceux-là seront à mes desseins propices,
> La victoire suivra mes pas, sous leurs auspices:
> Et je n'immoleray qu'à ma seule Vertu,
> Le Pirate François, à mes pieds abatu.
> Cependant je consens, que les Couples profanes,
> Immolez au Sultan, satisfassent ses Manes:
> Et que le deuïl puplic [sic] de l'Estat outragé,
> Par tes mains, par ton art, des Chrestiens soit vengé.
> Qu'on entende pourtant, que Forcadin n'estime,
> Que les Lauriers cueïllis dans un champ legitime:
> Et que sans tes Demons, de charmes soudoyez,
> Sans tes noirs armemens, des Enfers envoyez,
> Il sçaura bien venger, par sa seule vaillance,
> Le Croissant de la Croix, l'Egypte de la France.

(Book 13: p. 165A)

This is perhaps Forcadin's only moment of bad faith. However, Forcadin, even though he becomes generalissimo, is never truly in command of the Saracen camp. Those who are—Mélédin and Mirème—woo Fortune in any way they can. They are as Machiavellian as any of Corneille's villains, and, far more than in Tasso, particularly prone to deception, to fighting the Christians not by force of arms or will but through deceit. Hence a gift of poisoned armor to King Louis; hence two assassins dispatched to his camp, one in the guise of an ambassador, the other a tournament-challenger; hence Mélédin's honeyed words to convince Zahide that he must sacrifice her against his will.[22]

Le Moyne proposes as models for conduct neither the hero of will-to-power (Forcadin) nor the practitioner of Machiavellian cunning (Mélédin). On the contrary, Saint Louis discovers (Book 8) that the highest places in heaven are awarded to ascetics who have conquered the world in their own flesh (battles more glorious than on the field) and to martyrs who have submitted patiently to their fate. The prince of martyrs and, by extension, of ascetics as well, is Christ. And it is our highest duty to imitate him. Thus Le Moyne's protagonists fight inner battles, learning to renounce inglorious physical passion and the false worldly honors earthly love can bring, in favor of a more sublime religious life. King Louis and his princes follow the corpus Christi into Damietta, bareheaded and with bare feet, humbly weeping. And they are eager to die for God, to seek death in God. The crusader's true role is martyrdom, King Louis says, and the most glorious life is the shortest. As is often the case in the baroque period, religious heroism takes on a passive not active stance, is based on endurance not achievement, and manifests itself in resisting temptation rather than military conquest.[23] Yet Le Moyne resembles Corneille rather than d'Aubigné in that, for him, renunciation is triumphant, never tragic, and death is an instrument of realizing human potentiality, chosen not endured, allied to reason and not separated from it. For these people, renunciation (Bourbon,

---

[22] According to Gross-Kiefer, *Le Dynamisme cosmique*, Le Moyne's "false heroes," dominated by their passions, subject to doubt and anguish, manifest a Racinian rather than Cornelian psychology.

[23] See Frank J. Warnke, *Versions of Baroque: European Literature in the Seventeenth Century* (New Haven and London, 1972), chap. 8; Maskell, *The Historical Epic in France*, chap. 13.

Alégonde, Lisamante) and death (Robert, Lisamante, Belinde, Béthunes, and Raymond) are man's greatest achievements, opening the portals to heavenly bliss. There is only one crime possible in Le Moyne's world, though it may take sundry forms—apostasy; and only one virtue, from which all others derive—faith.

# 7  *Space, Time, and History*


In his *Dissertation du poëme heroïque* Le Moyne defends his choice of Louis IX as protagonist: Louis, a hero and saint, is more worthy of epic celebration than either Jason or Achilles and, in addition, he honors the royal house, France, and the French people.[24] Probably to emphasize Louis' overlordship in the Christian world, Le Moyne describes a marvelous pavilion sent to him by his relative the emperor of Constantinople (Book 1) and, in Book 5, pays particular attention to the Greek and Genoese contingents enrolled in the Christian host under Louis' orders. These men are led by a Greek philosopher and by a descendant of Byzantine emperors, eager to contribute to the victory of his holy French kin. This is a late manifestation of *translatio imperii et studii*, expressed more subtly but by no means less vigorously than in *chanson de geste* or Chrétien de Troyes. Like some other epic poets in his century, Le Moyne was an ardent patriot, who intentionally chose as his protagonist a renowned medieval historical figure (like Clovis, Charlemagne, and Joan of Arc), a national and religious hero.

Under Louis' banner are ranged contingents from all over Europe, Cyprus, the Christian Levant, and even Tartars from the Far East. Significantly, the troops participating in Louis' tournament pretend to represent distant climes: the burning South, the frozen North, and the wise East or heavenly Other World. On the Saracen side armies are dispatched from Egypt, the Saracen Near-East, Arabia, Persia, and Ottoman Turkey. In Book 18

---

[24] *Dissertation* [p. iii]: "je ne pouvois donc choisir un Heros plus accompli que celuy-là: et d'ailleurs le choix que j'en ai fait, est honorable à la France, qui l'a élevé; à nos Rois, qui sont nez de luy; à la Maison Royale, qui est de sa Race; à la Noblesse, qui l'a pour Patron et pour modele; à toute la Nation à laquelle Dieu l'a donné pour Protecteur; à toute l'Eglise, qui l'a receu au rang des Saints qu'elle revere."

38

Forcadin receives reinforcements from Themir, a King of the Steppes, ancestor of Tamerlane. The mustering of the troops (Books 5 and 9), an old Homeric and Virgilian convention, allows Le Moyne to proclaim the universality of his struggle, that, as in the *Song of Roland*, the entire world, Pagan and Christian, converges to give battle in an apocalyptic struggle between absolute good and absolute evil.

Although various battlefields are the focus of Le Moyne's universe, they do not dominate it exclusively, for even within Egypt, many an oasis or city remains apart from formal combat. On the one hand, we find great cities of the living (Damietta, Mansourah, Cairo) or the dead (the pyramids). This Saracen world is largely urban, depicted in terms of luxury, boundless wealth, and Oriental local color. We are expected to marvel before the splendor of the pyramids, Mélédin's barge descending the Nile, bedecked in silver and rubies, and the incredible wedding gifts he offers Lisamante (Book 13). Like Camoens, Tasso, Ercilla, Saint-Amant, and like the medieval *trouvères*, Le Moyne is intrigued by distant horizons and exotic landscapes; he too is not indifferent to the attraction of "L'Arabia Felice, albergo dell' aurora."[25] And, in specifically French terms, he shares the great burst of interest in the Modern Orient that erupted in the middle of the seventeenth century, that was to find its most striking literary manifestation in classical tragedy: plays such as Mairet's *Solyman* (1630), Tristan's *Osman* (1656), and, of course, Racine's *Bajazet* (1672).[26]

In contrast to the wicked Saracen cities, within this Satanic Other World are to be found two islands of calm, oases in the heart of nature consecrated to religious solitude. The first of these *loci amœni* is the area surrounding Aymon de Bourbon's tomb where his widow, the hermitess Alégonde, dwells:

> Les Prelats étonnez [. . .]
> Leurs yeux en sont surpris, et ne sçavent comment,

---

[25] *Dissertation* [p. viii]: "L'Egypte est le plus merveilleux de tous les Païs, et le plus fertile en grandes choses. Le Phare et les Pyramides, le Nil et le Caire, les Magiciens et les Monstres, les miracles de l'Art, et les prodiges de la Nature, sont originaires de ce Païs-là: Et les seuls noms des Sultans et des Sarrasins, remplissent l'oreille de leur son: la seule montre de leurs armes et de leur équipage surprend la veuë; et met dans l'esprit des images qui l'étonnent."

[26] On this question, consult Pierre Martino, *L'Orient dans la littérature française au XVIIe et au XVIIIe siècle* (Paris, 1906).

> La Nature a sans l'art produit tant d'agrément.
> Mais plus ravis encor de l'innocente haleine,
> Du Printemps eternel, qui regne en cette plaine;
> Ils prennent ce Vallon pour le Jardin fatal,
> Qui des premiers Humains fut le Païs natal.
>
> (Book 10: p. 121A)

The second recalls the apocryphal legend of the Matariya Fountain, where Mary is presumed to have washed the infant Christ's swaddling-clothes (Book 16). Following a topic which goes back to Antiquity (Horace's *Beatus ille* . . .), evil culture is set off against good nature. Le Moyne contrasts Saracen cities to these intimate, innocent holy places where a chosen elite aspires to enlightenment, to a life beyond the senses, where man may know God. This is the center, the sacred space, a temple within a sacred grove, tended by guardians of the cult, separate from the world and consciously set off against demonic parodies, the dead stone ruins of pyramids and Isis' temple. Here, following a "naturalist theology," particularly in favor with the Jesuit Fathers, beauty and harmony prove God's existence; indeed, God created the world for it to reflect him. Thus, it is here, in Christian solitude, that man converses through nature with God.[27]

Finally, as in *Les Tragiques* and, to some extent, *Moÿse sauvé*, phantoms and demons come to Egypt from the underworld, while Frenchmen rise spatially (they take to the high ground, the ruins of Joseph's palace, during the Nile flood), and their leader, who rises above the pyramids into another dimension, is wafted from earth to heaven. God's love flows down to man from above, and man yearns to soar up to where his creator dwells. There, in heaven, Louis views the whole world, East and West, from his celestial vantage point. And there past, present, and future meet. For, as Saint Michael instructs Louis in topography, he also reveals to him the history of the race. Geographical landmarks (Sodom and Gomorrah, Mount Ararat, Babel, the Red Sea, the Sinai Desert) are associated with sacred history; indeed, they took on a particular configuration at a moment in the past (sulphur flames,

---

[27] Cf. A. Kibédi Varga, "La Poésie religieuse au XVIIe siècle," *Neophilologus*, 46 (1962), 263-278.

ruins, traces of chariots and arms, or white bones) and have maintained that form ever since. The future as well as the past is inherent in the present, since Michael predicts future events—Charles of Anjou's exploits in Italy; an eventual conversion of the East by the Jesuit Order—also bound to particular *loci* in space. Up is good, down is evil. Satan and Adam fell, Christ descended but then rose to heaven on the third day. And the planet Earth is a battleground between heaven and hell.

According to Maskell, seventeenth-century long poems can be divided into three categories: the annalistic epic, the heroic epic, and the romance. Although Pierre Le Moyne chose to write in the second category, he was interested in history and hoped to be the Thucydides as well as the Homer of his age. He edited the Duc d'Estrées' *Memoires d'Estat* (1666), published a treatise, *De l'Histoire* (1670), and died in the midst of writing a history of the life and times of Cardinal Richelieu. In *La Sainte Couronne reconquise*, Le Moyne is eminently aware of other cultures in time and space, differing from his own, and of the passing of time and the imprint of the past. He paints a number of highly realistic historical frescos (a sea battle; landing operations) and makes an effort to deal with Mediterranean local color. He tries to show how previous events in time (the murder of Saladin's nine sons by Mélédin's father, the crusade expeditions in which Lisamante's father or Alégonde's husband participated) influenced Louis' crusade, and how the present conflict will give rise to future dynastic crises (the Mameluk rebellion that will dethrone Mélédin's line forever). An evil past of decadent idol-worship weighs heavily on the fortunes of Egypt, whereas the succession of good deeds, of gallant crusades, by Kings of France encourages Louis on the right path. Compared to his own seventeenth century, Le Moyne obviously prefers these virile, heroic, committed Christian knights.[28] Yet these great men of the past are happy to yield precedence to their descendants in Louis XIV's court, just as their ancestors in heaven were eager to give way to them. And Le Moyne, joyously taking up

---

[28] Cf. *La Gallerie des femmes fortes*, "La Carte de Paris," and *Dissertation* [p. vii]: "D'ailleurs, la Politesse, la Courtoisie, la Generosité, toutes les Vertus, toutes les Sciences amies des Graces estoient déja nées, estoient déja Françoises du temps de Saint Louïs. Les Vers, les Devises, les Tournois, estoient déja en usage: et la Chevalerie, comme on parloit de ce temps-là, estoit déja galante et spirituelle: mais galante sans desordre, et spirituelle sans libertinage."

an epic convention in Virgil, Ariosto, Tasso, and Ronsard, employs not only Louis IX and Bourbon but a host of minor figures to praise real and potential patrons of his work, seventeenth-century princes presumed to have descended from his doughty crusaders. Finally, when Le Moyne alters the facts of history, he does so out of patriotism and Christian faith. Like Virgil and Ronsard, he rejects annals in favor of myth. From his vantage point, he serves Clio by betraying her, for in his works history can be defined not merely as a collection of accurate facts but instead as a tradition of glory, the renown of great deeds in the hearts of men that come after, inspired and perpetuated by works of art. Thus the papal legate warns Saint Louis that kings ought not to be preoccupied with mere physical victories on the field of battle, but with other laurels, crowned in History:

> Et puis, ajoûte-t-il, les Testes souveraines,
> Qui regnent au dessus des Fortunes humaines,
> Sont d'un ordre trop haut, pour les petits Lauriers,
> Que la Gloire dispense au commun des Guerriers.
> Il en est de plus grands, et d'une autre matiere,
> Qui répandent au loin l'odeur et la lumiere:
> Et c'est de ces Lauriers eternels et luisans,
> Qui preservent les Noms de l'outrage des ans,
> Et font vivre les morts en honneur dans l'Histoire,
> Que vous doit couronner la main de la Victoire.

(Book 10: p. 117B)

People are buried, their names inscribed on a tomb, to await the glory of History, and Le Moyne, intruding in his own voice, promises "historical immortality" to Zahide and Muratan.

## 8 *Christian Typology*

Unlike other seventeenth-century writers of epic (Saint-Amant,
Scudéry, Chapelain, and Coras) it is probable that Le Moyne did
not intend an overtly allegorical interpretation for his poem.
Always so loquacious concerning his own works, he mentions
nothing of the kind in the *Dissertation du poëme heroïque* or in the
notes suffixed to each book of *Saint Louis*. Perhaps he believed
that his subject possessed such moral elevation and "universality"
as to require no further embellishment.[29] However, in my opinion, the epic does contain typological overtones.

The Christian notion of history is neither cyclical, as with the
Greeks and certain primitive societies, nor linear, based upon the
premise of continued progress, as in the modern period. Christian history is both linear and cyclical: it begins with Creation,
ends with Doomsday, and is organized according to a pattern,
with key events, such as Creation, the Fall, the Flood, Exodus, the
Crucifixion and Resurrection, and the Second Coming, playing
an essential role, dominating the flow of history and giving it sense
and structure. To the extent that certain events resemble each
other, that the consequences they unleash are in direct corre-
spondence or antithesis to the consequences unleashed by other
events, forces the Christian exegete to envisage a pattern of re-
currence, similar to that evoked by Mircea Eliade and given mean-
ing by symbolism rather than by pragmatic cause and effect.
Actions are important because they participate in transcendent
being and because each act imitates a divine archetype. In our

---

[29] Marni, *Allegory in the French Heroic Poem*, pp. 163-166. In fact, in the *Dissertation* Le
Moyne alludes slightingly to allegories, with reference to Tasso's alleged error in having
more than one hero in the *Liberata* [p. xi]: "De recourir à l'Allegorie, pour justifier cette
faute, comme a fait le Tasse, c'est faire venir de bien loin et à grands frais, une Chimere,
pour défendre une autre Chimere."

Christian world this tradition is represented by typological and allegorical interpretation of Scripture, that is, of sacred history, prevalent in the early Christian period, in the Middle Ages, and on into the modern world, a tradition that died out only in the nineteenth century. Nor should the notion of typology in the seventeenth century shock us. Pascal, Bossuet, Godeau, Desmarets, Marolles, and a host of baroque lyric poets all favored and/or practiced figurative readings of the Bible, and figurative symbolism is to be found in the *Josué* and *Samson* by Coras, in Saint-Amant's *Moÿse sauvé*, and in a Latin Moses epic which Saint-Amant and Le Moyne may have known, the *Moyses Viator seu imago militantis Ecclesiae* by Antoine Millieu, S.J. (1636-1639). Le Moyne and his contemporaries were also influenced by a new generation of scriptural commentators, favorably inclined toward typology, including Spanish Jesuits (Salmerón, Maldonado, Toletus, Ribera, and Pereyra) and the Belgian Cornelius a Lapide.

The crusaders are aware of their biblical heritage. Coucy the poet-musician sings stories from the Bible; on King Louis' armor are painted images of Old Testament heroes; and in heaven Louis is given a lesson in sacred history as well as geography. We are reminded again and again that the Egypt invaded by Louis' men is the land of Pharaoh as well as of Saladin. Mirème invokes demons in the pyramids and in a subterranean hall where Moses' rival magicians used to hold assembly; the crusaders seek refuge on a hill where the ruins of Joseph's palace lie; Brenne points out to Bourbon a series of geographical *loci* connected with the life of Moses, including the spot where, as an infant, his cradle was confided to the bullrushes (here Le Moyne probably was influenced by Saint-Amant's *Moÿse sauvé*). No wonder then that, addressing his troops, King Louis refers to how God succored Noah, Joseph, Moses, David, and Christ in the past and can do so again whenever he chooses. And, of course, God does choose to cast down Mélédin and Mirème as he did Pharaoh and Herod, and to exalt Saint Louis in the manner of Old Testament judges. Having died a martyr, like Christ, Robert d'Artois' body is wafted to the tomb of the Macchabees in Palestine so that, like Christ's, his physical remains shall not be discovered. Lisamante kills the Holophernes-Herod of her day and, Christ-like, walks on water. And God opens a passage for Louis' people across the waters as he did long ago for Moses. I further suggest that Le Moyne introduces the Flood-motif not only as a piece of Biblical local color but for its spiritual significance. In Prophets and Psalms it is said that since, in the time of Noah, God punished the mass and saved the remnant, he will do so again. In *Saint Louis*, whereas Noah and Moses delivered mankind from death by water, Christ will deliver us from fire in hell with the water of baptism. Analogies are established between Noah's ark, Moses' cradle, the ark of the covenant, and the Holy Sepulchre or the Holy Rood. And, of course, victory over the Flood also signifies Christ harrowing hell, defeating Leviathan in his own element. Louis and his men live in an intense, almost sacral present, yet also participate in the past and future. They march in the steps of their ancestors, spiritual as well as physical. They participate in the eternal crusade of Christ against Antichrist. *Milites Christi*, they imitate and postfigure the warrior who harrowed Hell and who delivered from bondage Moses, David, and the Macchabees. And they set an example for the Bourbon, Montmorency, Coligny, Condé, and Conti, in Pierre Le Moyne's day who, if they choose, can again beat back the Turk and win thrones in heaven through the crusade.

The analogies Le Moyne establishes between Mélédin and Pharaoh or Herod, between Louis IX and Christ or Moses, are not mere literary metaphors. Pharaoh persecuting Moses in the Old Testament prefigures Herod persecuting the infant Christ in the New Testament, an event which fulfills the type or figure. And (here Le Moyne extends the method to post-Biblical secular history, a less common but by no means unknown practice) both events are postfigured by Mélédin's persecution of Christians in the thirteenth century. All three episodes are united in a symbolic nexus, each existing historically in time but receiving its full significance only when the others are also taken into account. Le Moyne refuses traditional distinctions between sacred and secular or between pre- and post-advent history. For him, time includes all of history, and all moments of history contain the past and future consubstantial with the present. For the Christian, we live in an eternal present, for each moment of our lives is crucial to our own salvation and the future of mankind, and the present always refers back to the past and anticipates the future, containing past and future within itself.

The crusader host can be defined, in a larger sense, as God's elect, to be found in all places and times. And Satan the killer, the trickster, the rebel, an absolute foe without pity or pardon, is ever present with his minions to oppose them. Such was the case in the time of Pharaoh and Herod, as it is in the ages of Mélédin and of the Turkish sultans in Louis XIV's century. Thus the supernatural manifests itself in our everyday world. Perhaps of little intrinsic importance, people's lives assume significance with reference to the greater world of which they form a part, cosmic significance, since they are weapons in the service of higher powers. These events reflect divine will and are included in God's plan, because the Church, the central protagonist in history, abides in the past, present, and future.

## 9 Archetypes of Romance

Up to now, I have spoken largely of *Saint Louis* as a poem of convention, decorum, spectacle, and almost ritual high seriousness. In addition, it is many other things, being, like Tasso's *Gerusalemme liberata*, a highly complex work of art. Pierre Le Moyne shares with Tasso a predilection for romance. In Le Moyne's world a baby, attacked by a wolf, is then succored by an eagle and a tigress; heroes and heroines are captured by pirates and an innocent matron falsely accused of adultery; warrior maidens take to the field and, helmets down, duel their lovers in error; lovers perish together at the stake; and a brother and sister each seeks to die in place of the other. Knights give battle to giants, monsters, dragons, and fiends from hell. Sundry enchantments occur, in the tradition of late *chanson de geste* and the Italians: Pulci, Boiardo, Ariosto, and Tasso. These include poisoned armor and a poisoned crown of thorns, the Nile flood, an attack by fire-demons, walking on or passing through the Nile, magic water that heals wounds or saves souls, God's fire that destroys the aforesaid poisoned objects, and a host of illusory monster-demon obstacles. We must not forget that magic, whether white or black, was accepted as a natural facet of life in the seventeenth century. Thus conceived, the supernatural is not an adornment but an intrinsic part of the action, for, as in d'Aubigné, the entire universe takes sides for or against the crusaders, and, on the outcome of their battle, much of the future shape of the universe depends. Magic stood somewhere on the frontier between science and religion, between mysticism and technology. In literary terms, to dominate occult forces with enchantments was useful for suscitating *meraviglia* as well as a sense of mystery in the universe; it rendered *meraviglia* credible and allowed man's fascination with the occult to manifest itself freely.

This spectacular epic contains most of the archetypes of romance, and much of its plot (although in a complex and fragmented way) is based upon the quest pattern found in late *chanson de geste*, Arthurian romance, Homer, Virgil, and Tasso. The career of the romance hero has been summarized in the following terms: "A hero ventures forth from the world of common day into a region of supernatural wonder: fabulous forces are there encountered and a decisive victory is won; the hero comes back from this mysterious adventure with the power to bestow boons on his fellow man."[30] Thus Louis' crusade is envisaged as a quest for a sacred object, Christ's crown of thorns. Mirème and Mélédin invoke creatures from hell. Louis IX voyages to heaven, and Bourbon twice struggles with supernatural powers in a symbolic Other World. Louis, Bourbon, and the warrior-maidens submit to ordeals, defeat monsters, deliver captives, and commune with symbolic or real parent-figures (Louis VIII in heaven; Alégonde in her sacred retreat). Saint Louis, a sun figure with a holy nimbus, the ancestor of the sun-king Louis XIV, gives battle to the forces of darkness. Once a scapegoat, Robert, the king's younger brother, is sacrificed, the others proceed to victory, for Robert is a good *pharmakos*, sacrificed in Christ's name so that Christ's army will live. After these trials, the poem closes with total victory over the enemy, celebrated in three acts: conversion (Zahide and Muratan), marriage (Zahide to Brenne), and the coronation of Saint Louis with the Crown of Thorns, truly the greatest, most holy of treasures brought back to the homeland. And death-rebirth experiences—whether they take the form of a supernatural voyage, a battle with a dragon in dark woods, crossing the Nile, being wounded in battle and restored by miracle, or dying while one's soul is wafted to heaven—these occur in almost every book of the epic.

Unlike *La Chanson de Roland*, Le Moyne's crusader host contains no old men of note (with the exception of the blind Commander of the Templars, mentioned only in passing). No Nestor or Naimes stands by Louis' side; he is his own best adviser, or he takes counsel from the archangel Michael. Even though, when he voy-

---

[30] Joseph Campbell, *The Hero with a Thousand Faces* (New York, 1956 [1st ed., 1949]), p. 30.

ages to heaven, Louis speaks to his father, is guided by him and by Christ, yet, being the son of a great king, still in his youth, he is succored by God the Son, as if the *puer senex* quality of the Christian army is to be maintained on all levels, including the celestial. Add to this the fact that the good hermit, Tasso's vecchio d'Ascalona, has been transformed into a lady 200 years old but eternally young and beautiful, and that, although the Saracen enemy are depicted in terms of feminine imagery (subterranean halls, dragons, snakes, the Nile, etc.), Egyptian women are all young and benevolent. Evil is to be found only in their men. On the other hand, although Forcadin, the worthy descendant of Virgil's Turnus and Tasso's Argante, plays a splendid role in the Egyptian camp, the most memorable of the Saracens, their leaders and guiding spirits, are two horrifying greybeards, the Sultan and his sorcerer. Significantly, much of the poem recounts how young men and women, Pagan and Christian, seek to escape from the clutches of these two. Muratan tries to prevent Zahide's ritual sacrifice-execution by their father (Book 6). Judith comes from heaven to secure Lisamante from defilement by the same old man, while Béthunes weeps on the other side of the Nile (Book 13). Robert achieves his final victory over Drogasse, a father desperately eager to avenge the death of his son (Book 14). And, in order to work his way to the Matariya Fountain, Bourbon defeats a series of monsters, finally killing old Mirème in disguise (Book 16). It would appear that Le Moyne has consciously or unconsciously elaborated a pattern of Oedipal wish-fulfillment in which good young men and women defeat wicked old men with the help of supernatural sons and good mothers. And they mark their triumph over the fathers either with physical marriage on earth (Zahide and Brenne), spiritual marriage in heaven (Lisamante and Béthunes), or a coronation and the assumption of a father's role in turn, on earth (Louis) or in heaven (Robert). From Louis and Bourbon, as well as others, will sprout many a fair flower of France.

# 10 *Love and the Role of Woman*

Although Le Moyne has his youths triumph over their hoary adversaries, he does not permit many happy love-affairs. The Jesuit Father holds a most ambiguous attitude toward sexual love. On the one hand, *fin' amor*, in its baroque, post-Petrarchan, *précieux* form, runs through the epic. Again and again, youths and maidens tread on fire or ice, pierced by arrows, floods of tears bursting from their eyes. Zahide's suitors, princes and sultans all, are reduced to slavery by her eyes:

> Son nom estoit Zahide; et depuis le rivage,
> Où la Mer divisée à l'Hebreu fit passage,
> Jusqu'à cette autre rive, où le flot trémoussant,
> Se colore aux rayons du Soleil renaissant;
> Il n'estoit point de Cour soit barbare ou galante,
> D'où, des plus braves cœurs Zahide conquerante,
> N'attirast à Memphis, par bandes enchaisnez,
> Des Esclaves regnans, des Captifs couronnez.
>
> (Book 1: p. 3B)

Furthermore, on several occasions Le Moyne's heroes indulge in acts of flowery gallantry. Thus Charles of Anjou pointedly avoids an encounter with Zahide's and Almasonte's ship in the sea-war (Book 2); Zahide takes Lisamante prisoner, assuring her of the gentlest care and that her captors will fall in love with her (Book 12); when the two ladies duel on the battlefield, their respective suitors. Brenne and Béthunes, are eager to second them (Book 15); Brenne imagines using the Matariya water as a cure for Zahide not King Louis (Book 16); and after a fit of jealousy, he pays respect to her and to Cupid in his heart (Book 17).

On the other hand, throughout his works, Le Moyne condemns the evil effects of lust. In "Carte de la Cour" he excoriates the Palace of Gallantry; in "Avis salutaire à une illustre captive" he urges a lady to break her erotic chains; and "Laïs dechirée" is one of the most powerful evocations in all baroque literature of the horrors of misguided love. Furthermore, in his *Dissertation du poëme heroïque*, Le Moyne criticizes Virgil, Ariosto, Tasso, and Marino, all for having gone too far in the sympathetic depiction of Eros. Le Moyne will accept love as a convention in heroic poetry, but only in secondary episodes; furthermore, such love shall be depicted in pure, noble colors, and shall exist not as an end in itself but a means to an end, to inspire martial glory.[31] From both an ethical and an esthetic perspective, *amor* is deemed hierarchically inferior to *militia* and *caritas*.

Therefore, even though Le Moyne yields to convention, even though in certain episodes he follows the example of Tasso, on the whole Eros plays a sorry role in his epic. Four illustrious Moslems—Mélédor, Olgan, Alfasel, and Sultan Mélédin himself—commit cruel acts, in defiance of moral law, and are reduced to the level of beasts, all in the name of love. Dominated by their passions, by lust and jealousy, they become anti-heroes. Significantly, all four fail in their endeavors, indeed pay with their lives. God is not merciful to lovers in this poem; they fall in battle, dreaming of their ladies, with all their charms and erotic vows unable to help them. True, Brenne is dazzled by Zahide, and Bourbon by Almasonte, in somewhat the way Rinaldo adored Armida, and Tancredi Clorinda. However, as I said before (cf. p. 33 above), Brenne has practically no contact with Mélédin's daughter until she is on the point of converting to the Christian faith; and Bourbon's fascination with Almasonte is quickly dispelled by Alégonde's sermon and a miracle from heaven. At no time does either man become a love-slave in an equivalent of Armida's garden. Alégonde speaks out splendidly against erotic love. She

---

[31] *Dissertation* [pp. xv-xvii] and *Dichtungslehren der Romania*, p. 464: "Loin de ces Amours, les cajoleries, les mignardises et les mollesses, que le Tasse donne à son Renaud et à son Armide. Semblables choses sont pour les Amours vulgaires, pour les Amours des Colombes; et les Amours Heroïques sont des Amours d'Aigles. [. . .] Cela se verra dans la suite de ce Poëme, où l'Amour qui est la propre Passion des Heros, ne paroist point sur la Scene [. . .] qu'il n'y fasse quelque chose de noble et d'illustre, qu'il ne fournisse de matiere au Modele de quelque Vertu, necessaire ou bienseante aux Grands."

says that Bourbon cannot pluck laurels on the soft, decadent plain of love, but only on the mount of labor, glory, and virtue:

> Mais, Seigneur, ces Lauriers ne sont pas de ces plaines,
> Où se cueille la fleur des delices humaines.
> On ne les void point naistre en ces lieux enchantez,
> Où le Luxe nourrit les molles Voluptez:
> Où l'Amour, cette Abeille agreable et funeste,
> D'une courte douceur, fait une longue peste.
> Ils se doivent cueillir sur ces Monts escarpez,
> D'honorables sueurs, de sang noble trempez,
> Où bien loin du repos, bien plus loin des delices,
> Entre de hauts rochers, et de bas precipices,
> Par un sentier qu'on void de peu de gens battu,
> On arrive à la Gloire, en suivant la Vertu.
>
> (Book 11: p. 130A)

Man cannot be a slave and a master at the same time, for the chain of love leaves no place for a crown. Begin, she tells Bourbon, by conquering yourself! A child, Cupid vanquished you; you expect to kill a dragon yet you cannot even withstand this insect! Indeed, it is only by renouncing Almasonte that Bourbon wins the right to wear Aymon's armor and conquer the dragon.

In place of Eros, the author proposes another sort of relationship between the sexes, and in place of Armida other models for womankind. Raymond and Belinde, Aymon and Alégonde, Lisamante and her late husband, are proposed as exemplars of chaste Christian marriage. Indeed, Father Le Moyne places as much emphasis on chastity as on marriage. For these couples are evoked in terms that apply to a *mariage blanc*. Indeed, in Book 8, a special place in heaven is reserved for the chaste (Susanna, Judith, three *femmes fortes*) and for *mariés blancs*, including Saint Crispus and Saint Joseph. In the tournament (Book 4) Le Moyne gives preference to Platonic *fin'amor* (a flame that burns brightly without heat) and to the divine love that moves the spheres. Other such examples of abstemious, unsatisfied love are Béthunes' secret flame for Lisamante, and the pure, sibling affection between Zahide and Muratan.

That three *femmes fortes* are mentioned in the same terms as

Susanna and Judith, that Judith is shown to be the first and greatest scriptural *mulier fortis*, indicate to what an extent sexual purity and martial vigor are associated in Le Moyne's mind and how, on the other hand, unlike many clerics, his condemnation of *luxuria* does not develop into misogyny. On the contrary, he joyfully exploits the warrior-maiden tradition in Virgil (Camilla), Ariosto (Marfise, Bradamante), and Tasso (Clorinda, Armida). In *Saint Louis* we find two eminent *bellatrices* in the Christian camp and two (plus 100 others in the ranks) among the Saracens, all treated sympathetically. Belinde claims the right to fight in battle side by side with Raymond, for, a free person, she submits only to the laws of love and honor. Since love has taught her where lie the paths of glory, she and her husband will be immortalized together in History. King Louis grants her request, proclaiming that no sex is forbidden honor:

> Qu'elle vienne, dit-il, que cette Ame heroïque,
> Nous preste en ce combat, son exemple et sa pique:
> Qu'elle nous fasse voir, que la force est du cœur,
> Et qu'il n'est point de sexe éloigné de l'Honneur [. . .].
>
> (Book 10: p. 119A)

Then Judith, cutlass in hand, descends from heaven and convinces Lisamante to behead Mélédin, crying "Je viens à ton secours, Femme forte" (Book 13: p. 162B).

Le Moyne echoes a literary current prevalent in his day, especially in the 1640s—exaltation of the strong, domineering woman as a feminine ideal. Under the impact of contemporary political figures (Anne of Austria, Christina of Sweden, Louise-Marie of Poland, the Princess Palatine, La Grande Mademoiselle, and several duchesses active in the Fronde), influenced by heroic romance and *précieux* salons directed by ladies, and, of course, by the Bible, a series of treatises were composed on the subject, the four most notable being *Egalité des Hommes et des Femmes* (1622) by Montaigne's friend, Marie de Gournay, *Les Dames illustres* by Hilarion de Coste (1625), *La Femme heroïque* (1645) by Père Du Bosc; and *La Gallerie des Femmes fortes* (1647) by Père Le Moyne himself. This current was partially responsible for the fashion of

Judith, Esther, and Susanna as literary and artistic subjects and for a tradition of martial ladies in seventeenth-century epic.[32]

As Tasso does, Le Moyne expresses in glowing terms the fate of lovers separated by death. Lisamante and Dorisel, Alcinde and Léonin, Orasin and Mérinde, Bérenger and his wife, Coucy and his lady, Belinde and Raymond, Lisamante and Béthunes—they instill in the reader an intimate, truly Virgilian sense of *lacrymae rerum*. Tasso's idyllic-elegiac figures—Olindo, Sofronia, Erminia, Clorinda, Tancredi, even Armida—live again in the pages of Le Moyne. He feels pity for all unhappy lovers, even Saracens, for love undeclared or unrequited, forbidden or renounced, and for happy love cut short in its prime. This lyrical, subjective mood of pathos extends to nonamatory martyrdom, to the Christian children used as shields by the Egyptians and then burned at the stake, to Robert of Artois martyred inside Mansourah, flinging his blood in the air, a sacrifice to God. An atmosphere of foreboding pervades the epic. Like Tasso, Le Moyne is moved by the heroism of failure, the poetry of darkness and ruins, and man's anguish in the face of cosmic mysteries.

Thus, for all its beauty, life is full of illusion and deception: *Omnia vincit Mors*. All the reason more, cries the Jesuit poet, for man to renounce worldly glory and worldly love! In the last analysis, there is only one true love: the love of man for God and of God, principle of power, wisdom, and love, for man. God's love radiates from the center of his essence out to man, and man's love rises up to God. Le Moyne shares a neo-Augustinian, anti-Stoical doctrine rife in the seventeenth century (shared by the Dominican Coëffeteau and the Oratorian Senault) that love, illuminating reason and the will, directs our passions toward the Good. These passions, the sources of virtue and vice, are in themselves neutral. Their source and goal is love. They are surmounted not by reason and will but by love, a stimulus to glory. And, although Le Moyne is aware of mystical ecstasy (e.g., the ecstatic hermitess Alégonde), he is most attracted to Christian heroism, that is, to earthly love purified and transformed by divine love, by the celestial fire that is God (*Hymnes de l'amour divin*).[33]

---

[32] On this subject, consult R.A. Sayce, *The French Biblical Epic*, chap. 6.

[33] See Gross-Kiefer, *Le Dynamisme cosmique*, pp. 8-16; and André Stegmann, *L'Héroïsme cornélien, Genèse et signification*, Vol. 2 (Paris, 1968), pp. 236-237.

## 11  *Patterns of Demonic Imagery*

The opposition of forces, in Le Moyne's writings as in d'Aubigné's, is given expression in a pattern of antithetical demonic and apocalyptic imagery. Like d'Aubigné, like the Huguenot pastor Coras, this Jesuit father specializes in scenes of battle-horror, in the grizzly and the macabre. A Greek apostate, who brought the Crown of Thorns to Egypt, dies when molten gold is poured into his nose, ears, and mouth and his head is hung from a wall. After three days, a monstrous bird from the North, accompanied by 100 other black birds, carries away the dead man's remains (Book 1). Belinde dispatches an elephant, which, dying, falls on top of her, killing her in turn. At the same time, twenty Saracens are flung from a tower on the elephant's back and are struck down by their own weapons (a symbolic trophy to Belinde). The entire scene resembles a castle blown up from inside by sappers:

> Comme quand le Mineur, loin de l'air et du jour,
> Entreprend par le feu, d'enlever une Tour;
> Le tonnerre intestin, qu'il forme en ses entrailles,
> De leur chute, en grondant avertit les murailles:
> Puis avecque fracas, tout à coup éclatant,
> Et terrasse, cordons, ceintures écartant,
> Il mesle, d'une horrible et soudaine tempeste,
> Les poutres aux rochers, le fondement au faiste.
> Les Gardes malheureux, ou froissez au dehors,
> Ou brûlez au dedans, ont de bizarres morts:
> Et ce debris sanglant, de testes enlevées,
> De membres écrasez, et d'entrailles crevées,
> Est du Mineur surpris, et par sa mort vainqueur,
> Le triomphe et le deüil, la gloire, et le malheur.

> La pudique Heroïne ainsi fut opprimée [. . .]
>
> (Book 15: p. 191A & B)

These are only a few among many examples of horror in *Saint Louis*. The demonic, of course, extends to the Saracen people as a whole, to those men who dare take up arms against Christ, Shadow-figures, demons of the night. In the enemy camp are to be found a renegade, who planted around his house 100 pikes, on each of which is fixed the head of a Christian martyr; and a miscreant who cut the harnesses for six horses from Christians' skin and beats his battle drums with their bones. Dying, the man bites out and swallows the eyes of a Christian adversary, going to hell with blood on his hands and flesh in his mouth:

> Le cruel, en tombant retint sa cruauté;
> Et sur Imbaut mourant, par sa chute porté,
> A la Croix qu'il luy vid, renouvellant sa rage,
> Il luy mangea les yeux, luy rongea le visage;
> Et son Ombre feroce, aux Enfers descendant,
> Y fut le sang aux mains, et la chair sous la dent.
>
> (Book 14: p. 175A)

Such figures, who kill with passion and fury, with hatred for life and a thirst for blood, come close to the supernatural, in their ostentatiously absolute sadism. And, from time to time, the Saracen ranks are reinforced by even more impressive monsters: assorted giants, a lion, a crocodile, a hippopotamus, a dragon, and two squads of elephants. Most frightening of all, however, is the series of adversaries unleashed against Bourbon and Brenne when they undertake the quest of the Matariya Fountain: a giant, ten soldiers, a tornado of sand, a crocodile, a vision of hell, and a monster from the pit with the body of a dragon and head of a lion (Book 16). Serpent-imagery appears throughout the epic: enemies of Christian France, be they Mohammedans, Protestants, or Albigensians, are depicted as snakes and dragons. Thus Louis XIV vanquished the allegory *Discorde*, covered with snakes and armed with a "fronde" made of snakes. Louis IX speaks of the dragon of hell defeated by the Cross. Mirème's subterranean hall, where Moses' adversaries created serpents, is supported by pilasters entwined by sculptured stone vipers. The dragon's blood poisons the vegetation, while Saint Louis almost perishes from poisoned armor and from the wound of a poisoned arrow. These serpent-figures all recall the Prince of Darkness who deceived Adam and Eve but who was and will be deceived in turn, at the beginning and end of time, by dragon-slayers, Michael and Christ, Saint Louis' patrons.

In Book 12 the Moslem dragon slays with his blood as well as his venom. And death, whether from water or other causes, results in the shedding of blood. Both blood and natural water serve as demonic images in Le Moyne's epic. The ill-fated Lisamante was born in her parents' blood: her mother dies in childbirth, her father in a Saracen ambush. The shade of Saladin demands the blood of one of Mélédin's children to expiate the blood of his own nine sons, murdered by the Sultan's father. If this blood is cast into the Nile, the waters will rise; otherwise, Cairo's blood will flow at Christian hands. Mélédin accepts Saladin's conditions, thus fulfilling Muratan's mocking, pathetic request that the Sultan kill Zahide himself, washing his crown in her blood:

> Et bien, dit-il, enfin, puisqu'il est arresté;
> Et que l'arrest du Sort veut estre executé;
> Que Zahide perisse, et que des Ombres vaines,
> Viennent boire à tes yeux le beau sang de tes veines:
> Assouvis t'en toy-mesme, et join Pere inhumain,
> Le crime de la langue à celuy de la main.
> De ta main, de ton sang ta Couronne lavée,
> Sans tache et sans déchet, te sera conservée [. . .]
>
> (Book 6: p. 67A)

The Nile then does flood; this *verkehrte Welt*, a floating tomb, a desert of water drowning the trees, is no less horrifying than the storm at sea which capsizes two of Alphonse's ships. It is an image of sudden, violent, and irresistible death. Some of Le Moyne's other works evoke the sea in terms of gentle revery or as a mirror reflecting inconstancy, the evanescence of the world in contrast to God's power ("De la Vie champestre," "Le Speculatif," "Acteon"). However, it is the return to chaos, the unleashing of evil waters, that stands out in *Saint Louis* as in Saint-Amant's *Moÿse sauvé*. The irregular, tumultuous change in the sea, a storm or flood, a sudden transformation from calm to fury, violent metamorphosis—these command our astonishment. And the confusion of the four elements, the unleashing of water in the place of fire, air, and earth, is an image of chaos, of the negative power of Satan, enemy of God, rebelling against God's order.

Of course, fire can be unleashed along with water. Perhaps Mirème's greatest feat of wizardry is the assault of fire-demons against the Christian camp (Book 13). A rain of fire and lightning, assisted by the sorcerer's own canons, almost destroys the crusade then and there:

> Le feu se prend au Pont, aux Tours, à la Levée;
> L'onde en est elle-mesme à peine preservée;
> Elle écume, elle siffle, et par son sifflement,
> Ou s'irrite, ou se plaint de l'ardeur qu'elle sent [.]
> Mais elle en siffle en vain, en vain elle en écume,
> Son ennemi vainqueur de son dépit s'allume:
> Et contre elle échauffé, contre elle s'élevant,
> Encore à son renfort appelle-t-il le vent.

> (Book 13: p. 166B)

In this situation, as with the Nile inundation, the four elements break out of their confines, and the world is plunged "upside-down." The dragon ultimately vanquished by Bourbon is also a fire-creature, with flaming eyes and tongue; Raymond's mother is threatened with death at the stake; and the poisonous suit of armor sent by Mélédin to Louis contains fire but kills without visible flame. Finally, Mirème invokes demons with a sulphurous torch in hand (Books 5 and 16) and creates for Bourbon a vision of the pit, a river of fire and blood that torments a thousand souls:

> A ses yeux étonnez, il s'offre un gouffre ouvert,
> Un gouffre dont les bords ne portent rien de vert:
> Peu de troncs secs et noirs, sans bras et sans feuïllage,
> Font un funeste atour à son triste rivage.
> L'épouvantable gouffre à rez-de bord est plein,
> D'un fleuve limonneux, rouge de sang humain:

> Le feu s'y mesle à l'onde, et l'onde fugitive,
> Roule sans intervalle alentour de sa rive.
> Là mille malheureux haut et bas agitez,
> Et des vagues, du feu, du limon tourmentez,
> Flottent, comme l'on void le debris d'un naufrage,
> Sur la mer en courroux, flotter durant l'orage.
>
> (Book 16: p. 204B)

These flames that create martyrdom, as in *Les Tragiques*, also symbolize the degrading passions (Mélédin's lust, Forcadin's choler) that unleash violence, find an outlet in destruction, and thus mark Satan's presence among men.

Although, unlike d'Aubigné, Le Moyne does not evoke castles or prisons, he does create a striking pattern of religious and funereal architecture. The sun and stars sparkle on the summit of the great pyramid, and fires of hell burn from beneath. In this desert of solitude, the pyramids and the mummies they contain are fit only for the dead; mountains of pride created by man from the sweat and tears of poor slaves, they memorialize past grandeur (Book 5). These Bachelardian images of hard earth, of the triumph of the will, are juxtaposed to a complementary demonic pattern of soft earth, rot, stench, excrement, and decay. I am thinking of the crocodile's grotto in Damietta (Book 3) or the ruins of Isis' temple, both of which are filled with skeletons, blood, intestines, darkness, and pestilence (Book 12); and of Pharaoh's subterranean hall, where pilasters of bronze are embellished by monster-masks, snakes, and hideous figures, ruins now inhabited by owls, dragons, and ghosts:

> Ce lieu toûjours depuis des Hommes detesté,
> Des Hiboux, des Dragons, des Spectres habité;
> Fait paslir le Soleil, fait horreur à son ombre:
> Et toûjours pestilent, toûjours noir, toûjours sombre,
> N'a point d'autre clarté, que celle qu'y répand,
> Le regard d'une Orfraye, ou celuy d'un Serpent.
>
> (Book 16: p. 197B)

Like Théophile, Tristan, and Saint-Amant, Pierre Le Moyne enjoys depicting grotesque, macabre landscapes, with ruins, swamps, owls, skeletons, and ghosts. He partakes of a fascinating current of "pre-romantic" horror in the seventeenth century. Yet he never allows us to forget that these buildings are a pagan heritage, fixed in immobility and silence, that man's ambition leads only to the grave: *sic transit gloria mundi* (Book 9). Whether conceived as "hard earth" or "soft earth," castle, hall, temple, tomb, and grotto lie at the center of Le Moyne's demonic world. Ideally, such edifices should be sacred temples, set in an isolated, sacred space, *loci amœni* tended by guardians of the cult, devoted to enlightenment. Ideally, they should be "points of epiphany," intersecting heaven and earth, reserved for communion with God. Instead, associated with or decorated by twisting snakes, all of these buildings evoke a maze, a wasteland of disorder, inhabited by the dragon, hideous caricatures of what true temples ought to be.

In *la Gerusalemme liberata* night-time can suscitate a mood of nostalgia and elegy, of repose in the quiet of a friendly, intimate cosmos. Such is practically never the case in *Saint Louis*. For Le Moyne, the setting of the sun is an invitation for Satan to act. After dark, Mirème invokes the dead and performs his black mass; Mélédin sacrifices his daughter; the Nile rises; Forcadin and Zahide invade the crusaders' camp; Bourbon faces a phantom attack; and fire-spirits burn the bridge. And it is at night that the Frenchmen hear cries of horror and behold flames in the sky, discovering only the next day that the Christian minority in Damietta has been massacred:

> La Lune s'avançoit [. . .]
> Quand des cris de frayeur, et des voix de menace,
> Telles qu'on les entend au sac de quelque Place,
> De leurs tristes accens rompent nostre repos,
> Et réveillent au loin les Vents et les Echos.
> Les Echos et les Vents en trouble leur répondent:
> Du rivage prochain les vagues les secondent:
> Et les vagues, les Vents, les Echos et la Nuit,
> Font un concert d'horreur, de tumulte et de bruit.
>
> (Book 3: p. 31B)

These muffled, foreboding sounds contribute as much to the mood of terror as do flames and darkness. So in the midst of a night-sortie the reader is struck by an echo of exotic Saracen musical instruments, tumult, the neighing of horses, and howling of the dying. And people hear the dragon hiss and the noise of falling trees and rocks before the monster comes into view. Darkness and noise are two factors that accompany the enchantments unleashed upon Saint Louis' men; they help invoke a vision of chaos and evil, of *verkehrte Welt* in all its terrifying cosmic finality. And this darkness symbolizes a spiritual blindness on the part of Saracens, who fail to see God on earth, are myopic, and dazzled by false, worldly glitter.

# 12  *Patterns of Apocalyptic Imagery*

Satan tricks us with worldly honors then destroys us through war and black magic. He commits crimes against nature (turning the four elements from their proper functions), against man (inciting war, injustice, and sexual vice), and against God (Mirème's witchcraft and blasphemy). However, the authors of *verkehrte Welt* are not victorious; in this cosmic struggle of good versus evil, God ever maintains a *concordia discors*, against which their disruptive efforts prove futile. Demonic hard imagery of the will is nullified or transformed from evil to good. Thus when Alcinde slays the Satanic crocodile of Damietta at the door of a mosque, two towers and the mosque's dome collapse. God not only destroys the evil, poisoned armor sent from Mélédin to Louis; he replaces it by another, finer suit of armor handed down from Alégonde to Bourbon. (This scene may also allude to the fact that Bourbon's line will ultimately replace King Louis' on the throne of France.) The evil tombs of Pagans and Saracens are set in opposition to the good sepulchre, located in a terrestrial paradise reflecting the heavenly one, which will house the bodies of Aymon and Alégonde uncorrupted until Doomsday. Next to the sepulchre lies a beautiful piece of rock, with fire and water above it, descended from heaven, an image of God.

Mélédin will do anything to defend his throne, including the murder of his daughter, but he will perish, his dynasty with him, and Saracen thrones and altars will be transformed into pedestals for the Cross. On the other hand, Louis' and Bourbon's families will rule France forever. A flying machine, in the form of a throne, cleansed in fire, takes Louis to heaven where he beholds Christ's throne and the throne he himself will occupy there one day. Similarly, the pagan altar, used to sacrifice Zahide, fails in its function, is nullified by the throne that she also is promised in heaven (Book 17) and by good Christian altars: the holy altar with the eucharist rolled into Damietta (Book 3); the spectacular tournament altar with a burning phoenix drawn by unicorns and guided by a virgin (Book 4); and the altar of heaven, to which an angel brings Saint Louis' tears (Book 8).

Pierre Le Moyne also contrasts lifeless pagan stone to manifestations of nature in the green world. At Aymon's tomb and at the Matariya Fountain, demonic imagery yields to the pastoral, the sword to flowing water, and Armida's garden is transformed, purified, and redeemed. The vegetable world contributes to a pattern of salvation, negates or rectifies the more savage, demonic pattern of the mineral world, thus the *locus amœnus* contrasts with the city or the temple. These pleasances are assimilated to all that is beautiful, good, and true, to our dreams of a lost Eden and to our hopes for eternal rebirth in a new one. Earthly power and the chains of mortal sin yield to Christ's crown of thorns. Offered the crowns of the Holy Roman and Byzantine-Oriental empires (emblems of power and riches), Louis chooses the symbol of Christ's passion, kisses it, and places it on his head (Book 8). This holy diadem protected the Saracen throne as long as it was housed in Cairo; with its capture, Mélédin's House falls, and the thorns will protect the Capetian and Bourbon crowns of France. The poem ends with Louis' coronation, when the crown miraculously places itself on his head:

> D'elle-mesme de là, vers Louïs s'avançant;
> Et sur son front baissé, tout à coup s'abaissant,
> Tandis que d'allegresse au loin le Camp resonne,
> Des peines et du sang de son Dieu le couronne.
>
> (Book 18: p. 234B)

This crown is associated with other holy crowns (the circle of palm trees that surrounds Alégonde's earthly home, a chaplet of flowers awaiting her in heaven) and with the Holy Cross. For, when in heaven, King Louis chooses Christ's thorns over the empires of Rome and the Orient, he also requests his cross and nails:

Aux épines, Seigneur, si vous joignez vos cloux,
Les liens en seront plus fermes et plus doux:
Et vostre Croix pour comble, à vos cloux ajoustée,
Tiendra d'un poids plus fort mon amour arrestée.
Heureux si prés de vous à la Croix attaché,
Je puis de vostre sang nettoyer mon peché!
Et plus heureux encor, si vos flames divines,
S'allument dans mon cœur, sous ces saintes épines!

(Book 8: pp. 91B & 92A)

In Book 1 Le Moyne invokes Christ's crown of thorns on the altar of the cross, and in Book 9 he tells how Christ, stretched on wood, killed the Serpent and with bloody nails forged keys to the kingdom of heaven. It is appropriate, then, that Bourbon place his trophy, the head of the slain dragon, under the Cross, Christ's tree, that redeems Adam's Tree of the Knowledge of Good and Evil (Book 12).

Finally, Le Moyne speaks of the laurel as an image of heroism, of the palm branch as an image of martyrdom, and, above all, of the French *fleur-de-lis*. He declares that King Louis' victory will result in a grafting of the crown of thorns onto the crown of lilies, the *fleur-de-lis* ensuring that Louis' descendants will sprout on the royal tree and that future kings and kingdoms shall put their names beneath the names of Louis' and Bourbon's descendants (Books 1 and 8). And he praises Julie de Montausier, daughter of his patrons, the Marquis and Marquise of Rambouillet, who will bloom on the family tree and, crowned by myrtle, be allied with the *fleur-de-lis*. Christ and the French royal house are assimilated, for the lily, the emblem chosen by Clovis for his purification through baptism, stands for the Virgin Mary and the annunciation of Christ's coming as well as for the Capetian-Bourbon dynasty. The triumph of the green world requires the feminine principles of fertility, growth, and a natural organic order to prevail over flame and stone. The Saracens may be sterile, but the French partake of, and participate in, nature; as God's chosen people, they are close to the forces that bring life and order, and they are assimilated to them. And theirs is a family, a line of descendants, a genealogical tree comparable to the Tree of Jesse that extends from Adam to Christ, who restored the Tree of Life with his Cross. Through the image of the tree this sacred line is assimilated to the innocence of the pastoral in nature.

Although lilies and the crown of thorns risk being uprooted by the Nile flood, this Satanic inundation is paradoxically curbed by water. Saint Michael bears King Louis' sighs and tears to heaven in a vase (a scene perhaps inspired by Jocabel's weeping in *Moÿse sauvé*), then returns to earth to announce to the saint-king: "Your tears have dammed the Flood!" (Book 8: p. 86B). Man can offer another sacrifice to God, more meaningful than tears, however. Martel, killed in place of Louis IX, and Robert of Artois cast their blood into the sky, offering it to Christ, who gave his blood to us. Louis prays to God that since Christ's blood flowed to save us, he can surely stop the Satanic flow of the Nile. And Bourbon offers joyfully to water his laurels with his own blood (Book 16) upon setting out on a quest for the Matariya Fountain. This semi-divine water cures Louis' and Zahide's wounds and thrusts Zahide onto the path of conversion. Image of life, truth, and grace, the fount of all good, the Matariya water cures bodies and souls, purifies and renews life.

Just as water flows over Alégonde's rock, an image of temptation spurned, fire burns upward, inspiring her to meditate on heaven. An angel declares:

> Pour éteindre l'Enfer, et noyer ses supplices,
> Pour embraser le Ciel, et brûler ses delices,
> Pour reduire à moy seul, vos craintes et vos vœux,
> Je vous laisse ces eaux, et vous laisse ces feux.
>
> (Book 10: p. 125A)

The Saracens burn Christians at the stake, but to no avail, for their fire as well as the profane flame of lust can be purified whenever God wishes. A martyr-wife points out to her husband that the sparks of the stake will form a dais for their seats in heaven (Book 13), and Raymond proclaims over Belinde's corpse that the flame of their love is such that their ashes will be buried in the same grave and their souls will shine like one flame in heaven:

> Nous eusmes en commun, la vie et la fortune,

> Il restoit que la mort, nous fust aussi commune:
> Et que de nostre amour, dont le feu fut si beau,
> La cendre se meslast en un mesme tombeau.
> Qu'elle y soit donc meslée; et qu'aprés cette vie,
> De l'Hymen eternel de nos ames suivie,
> Bien-tost nous ne soyons, et morts, et glorieux,
> Qu'une cendre sous terre, et qu'un feu sur les Cieux.
>
> (Book 16: p. 196B)

In a sort of baptism of fire, King Louis is taken to heaven on a flaming throne. And God's lightning, by divine miracle, twice intervenes (Books 10 and 18): once to burn away Louis' poisoned armor (cf. the burning fiery furnace in the Book of Daniel) and later to destroy the false crown of thorns, infected with the plague. Thus the demonic flame of choler and lust can be redeemed by divine inspiration, prophecy, faith, ecstasy, purification, eternal life, the only mediation between heaven and earth (the Holy Spirit), cosmic power of creation, and God's truth and love—all embodied in fire.

Louis IX, the sun of his court, bestows light and order onto his entourage, who owe their very being to him. Here Pierre Le Moyne assimilates the historical saint-king to his descendant, the sun-king of the seventeenth century, Louis XIV. Similar political sun-imagery is to be found in "Le Soleil politique," "Le Ministre sans reproche," and *De l'Art de regner*. Furthermore, the sun emanating from the saint-king, Louis, is assimilated to the five suns of the stigmata on the body of heaven's king, Jesus Christ (Book 8). With one ray of light from Michael, a dying Robert of Artois becomes as strong as an eagle in spring (Book 14). Indeed, throughout the poem Christian light triumphs over Saracen darkness. Thus, before the capture of Damietta, a circle and crown of light from the sun stand over the crusader fleet, while at night a cloud with a white cross flies over the setting crescent moon (Book 3). And Zahide has a vision in which Mary's hand and eye bring her light, and the sun again triumphs over a crescent moon (Book 17). Physical light and the act of seeing are images of spiritual or moral insight granted to the Christian host, in contrast to Saracen blindness. God and his angels are forces of light, while Satan and his minions hide in darkness. The shadow of spiritual death, hell, sorcery, and vices contrasts to the light that emanates from Christ, the Tree of Jesse, and the *fleur-de-lis*. For Le Moyne, the earth is often shrouded in night, but heaven is based in pure light, for fire and light are images of divine power, wisdom, and love. They destroy or transform, act as eternal wrath no less than as eternal grace, and they overcome the false light of human worldliness. In the second "Amour divin" the poet invokes the Holy Spirit, who as fire spoke to Moses in the Burning Bush. Love is conceived as God's own vital principle, created from the flames of the Father and Son. It is the embodiment of divine creation and generation, and of his grace offered to sinners. The stars represent angels hovering around the divine sun, flying mirrors reflecting God, and human souls too, for Christ on the cross is a torch whose sparks light up the world.

As with d'Aubigné, the triumph posited by Pierre Le Moyne—of fire over fire, of water over water, and of flowers over stone—can be explained only in terms of Christian paradox. Louis IX's tears suffice to dam the flood of the Nile in the same way that a few drops of Christ's spilt blood broke the doors of hell and drowned Satan's demons. The only riches that Louis seeks in Egypt are a handful of miserable thorns. If he had sought more, he would have been defeated a hundred times, but since he seeks thorns, he will win the treasures of the Orient and, because of this pitiful, ironic crown, the crown of France will remain in his family forever. A uniquely spiritual prize ensures material as well as spiritual rewards. And dead, sterile thorns alone provide fertility and health, both in the Egyptian wasteland and in France's blessed garden. Similarly, this glorious conqueror walks humbly, barefooted, behind God's altar, ready for defeat whenever God wills it. Since he welcomes martyrdom, Louis always triumphs; because he proclaims that the greatest victory is to suffer, he never fails. In Book 9, Michael tells Louis that because of Christ's death all deaths died to life:

> Voy tirant vers le Nord cette seche colline,
> Qui se montre de haut à la Cité voisine.
> C'est le sacré Theatre, où la Vie à la Mort,
> S'unit par un fatal et solennel accord:

> Où de la mort d'un seul tous les Morts revescurent;
> Et d'une seule mort toutes les morts moururent.
> C'est là que l'homme-Dieu sur le bois attaché,
> Ecrasa le Serpent, étouffa le Peché;
> Et que des cloux sanglans, qui les mains luy percerent,
> Les clefs des Cieux fermez, par l'Amour se forgerent.

> (Book 9: p. 104B)

Louis undergoes symbolic death more than once, and, therefore, he lives. He imitates Christ, chooses his master's crown, and thus becomes worthy of being Christ's deputy in the world.

# 13  Communication, Language, and Art

Le Moyne's attitude toward verbal communication and the world of art is most ambivalent. Saracens often use language for evil purposes, to deceive good people, and many of his finest orators deliver splendid Cornelian tirades on Satan's behalf. For Christians and for "good" Saracens who have not yet converted, speech often proves to be futile; in any case, these crusaders do not rely upon words in order to communicate. Zahide was tricked by her father into accepting death, yet neither she nor Muratan can convince the other which one should die (Book 6). The papal legate cannot make Louis see why he ought not to fight the dragon. Only fire from heaven will bring the saint-king to abandon this particular ordeal (Book 10). Similarly, when Alcinde kills the Damietta crocodile and Léonin joins her in martyrdom, language is of no use to them. Significantly, Olgan's speech fails to touch Alcinde, she deigns not to address him, and it is only when he perceives a loving glance directed from her to Léonin that he realizes she loves another. He speaks but again to no avail, and she perishes at his hand:

> Alcinde avec mépris et d'un air genereux,
> Répond de son silence au barbare amoureux:
> Et vers moy se tournant, d'un geste de tendresse,
> Interprete muet du cœur qui me l'adresse,
> M'asseure de nouveau des gages de sa foy,
> Et me jure des yeux, qu'elle mourra pour moy.
> Olgan qui le remarque, en entre en jalousie:
> Une obscure vapeur trouble sa fantaisie:
> Et de son cœur piqué d'un funeste serpent,
> L'enflure avec horreur sur son front se répand.

> D'un ton de furieux, et d'une voix coupée,
> D'autres feux, luy dit-il, ton Ame ont occupée [. . .]
>
> (Book 3: pp. 34B & 35A)

Conversions are brought about not through exhortation but from a supernatural vision, the result of divine grace, and King Louis sees the future of his line projected onto heavenly space. The Christians know what they want to do, and they do it. Communication is totally unnecessary between these committed, militant, essentialist heroes, whose destiny is plotted out in advance. Verbal discourse plays a serious role only on three levels: prophecy (Alégonde or Michael informing Bourbon and Louis of the future), exhortation to inferiors (Louis' tirades to restore the courage of his troops), and prayer. Louis' eloquent, heart-felt prayers derive from the Jesuit *oraison*. One of the major contributions of Jesuit spirituality, beginning with Ignatius of Loyola himself, was the importance given to cultivating personal familiarity with God through the regular practice of intense oral and mental prayer.[34]

Esthetic makers of language—that is, poets and singers—do play a role in the epic. Aware of the story recounted in the thirteenth-century romance *Le Châtelain de Coucy*, Pierre Le Moyne tells of a brave knight, gallant lover, and poet, named Coucy. Coucy sings stories from the Bible, is responsible for entertaining the host with fireworks, and it is he who recounts to the Acre contingent Louis' adventures during their absence. The other *nuntius* in the poem, who tells Louis of Alphonse's exploits, an anonymous "delegate" in the 1653 version, in 1658 becomes Béthunes, Lisamante's unhappy suitor. May not Le Moyne have discovered the medieval *trouvère* Conon de Béthunes and set him parallel to the *trouvère* Guy de Coucy? Presumably, he had already confused the latter with Raoul II, Lord of Coucy, mentioned by Joinville, who indeed perished in battle at Mansourah. In any case, Béthunes and Coucy are fine crusaders, a credit to their country and their line. However, it should not be forgotten that both men are associated with profane, erotic love, and both perish on the field. Poets fall in battle; their artistic powers are as useless to them as is requited love.

[34] See Joseph de Guibert, S.I., *La Spiritualité de la Compagnie de Jésus, Esquisse historique* (Rome, 1953), chap. 14.

We find in *Saint Louis* a profusion of art-objects and of functional objects transformed into works of art: armor, pavilions, castle walls, thrones, tombs, even a basin. Le Moyne relishes in these magnificent "things" as sheer spectacle. However, from his perspective, art, like Eros, is a neutral entity. Entirely dependent upon the moral quality—vice or virtue—that inspires it, it can be devoted to good or evil. Some are morally commendable works of beauty: the Byzantine tent, the ruins of Joseph's castle, Louis IX's throne in heaven, and Aymon de Bourbon's tomb, among others. These all depict, in the form of frescos, sculptures, or tapestries, events from sacred history or miraculously predict the future history of France; they preserve from oblivion great deeds committed in the past and encourage men to perform equally great deeds in the present. On the other hand, the Saracen world contains no less beautiful but morally corrupt monuments: poisoned armor, pyramids, the ruins of ancient temples and altars, mummies, and a coffer containing the two crowns of thorns. God's fire destroys the suit of armor and the coffer, and a fire lit by Zahide destroys Bourbon's tent, thereby consuming the painted glory of Antiquity.

Pierre Le Moyne has a high opinion of his own standing as an artist. In his *Dissertation du poëme heroïque* he cites commendable examples from Homer, Virgil, Tasso, and himself. His ambition is to instruct princes,[35] to be an Aristotle to the Alexanders of his age. He shall instill in them heroism and grandeur of soul, teach them how to make war and to reign. Like Ronsard, he shall be a mediator for his patrons, just as, in his poem, Michael, Mary, and Alégonde mediate between crusading heroes and the mysteries of heaven. Furthermore, the Jesuit poet always places art in the service of morality and religion. Like Milton and Saint-Amant, he proclaims the duty of the Christian poet to use his "talent" for God, as a sacrificial offering, and to write with austerity, discipline, and responsibility. Art is good when it tells of God's eternal glory, evil when it upholds pagan or sensuous-materialist interests. For Le Moyne, poetry must be guided by reason, receiving its inspiration from angels in heaven, not a fictional Parnassus. Since

---

[35] *Dissertation* [p. xx]: "La perfection des Grands est la fin de la grande Poësie: le Poëte n'y peut contribuer que des Modeles de sa façon: et l'usage de ces Modeles est de purifier les Passions les plus ordinaires aux Grands: il est de former en eux, les Vertus les plus necessaires aux Personnes de leur condition."

the world is fundamentally good, the poet has only to recreate the natural order of the universe, acting in harmony with the world and with God. If he is sufficiently inspired his poetry will generate spiritual love, and he himself be drawn to heaven. Indeed, in this way he can imitate God and create in the image of the Creator, close to the world of pure spirit.[36]

[36] For Le Moyne's "philosophy of art," consult Gross-Kiefer, *Le Dynamisme cosmique*, pp. 61-75; and Ulriksen, "Pierre Le Moyne—poète baroque français," pp. 23-26.

## 14 *Final Estimate: "Saint Louis" in the Seventeenth Century*

*Saint Louis, ou la Sainte Couronne reconquise* is an uneven work. The modern reader will be repelled by the more conventional or topical scenes in Le Moyne's poem: I am thinking of Lisamante's romantic childhood, the tournament, and the lengthy foreshadowing of modern French history. However, where Le Moyne is at his best—and this turns out to be a surprisingly high proportion of the total work—he is magnificent. In descriptions of a storm at sea, of naval and land battles, of demonic, decadent landscapes, in the psychology of jealousy and will-to-power, in scenes of martyrdom and love-death melodrama—here Le Moyne surpasses all but the greatest of his contemporaries. No less impressive is the richness and complexity of a poem containing such extraordinary juxtapositions of style, theme, and tone. Le Moyne includes in his masterwork epic, lyric, war, romance, horror, extravagance, melodrama, and mystical ecstasy. A mixture of Tassian *mirabile* and *patetico*, of *furore* and *concetti*, could hardly please Boileau's generation, but it corresponds admirably to a more recent romantic and even surrealist esthetic. A public capable of appreciating this Jesuit Father only now has come into being centuries after his death.

In spite of historical inaccuracy and close dependence on a preceding epicist (Torquatto Tasso), Pierre Le Moyne may well have succeeded in writing the finest French *poëme heroïque* in the neo-classical mode. In fact, with the exception only of *Les Tragiques* and perhaps *Moÿse sauvé*, Le Moyne's *Saint Louis* proves to be the most successful serious long poem in French in the period extending from Jean de Meun or Guillaume de Machaut up to Lamartine and Hugo. His epic is redolent with splendor, spectacle, and grandeur, illustrating the themes of *mundus theatrum*, metamorphosis, reality and illusion, and order and chaos. In Le Moyne's patriotic Christian universe, man proves to be an essentialist being, manifesting deeds of superhuman heroism and joyfully submitting to martyrdom at will, God's grace always with him. But this is also a world of magic and terror, of sorcerers and fair maidens, where the entire crusader host and its individual leaders undertake a quest in the finest medieval tradition of romance. The cosmic struggle between good and evil is depicted through an extraordinarily complex pattern of antithetical imagery: Satanic horror, monsters, serpents, blood, water, fire, demonic architecture, and night, which oppose but inevitably give way before Christian beauty, blood, water, fire, natural growth (the crown of thorns, the cross, the *fleur-de-lis*), and the light of the sun. Right wins out over might in this poem of wish-fulfillment for the seventeenth-century aristocracy and militant clergy.

Scholars ascribe some of the traits I have found in Pierre Le Moyne's epic—illusion, *trompe-l'œil*, paradox, metamorphosis, theatricality, spectacle, ostentation, horror, concrete delight in the world, multiple sense imagery, the distortion of reality, and exaggeration—to the baroque mentality taken in a very general sense. Yet, several aspects of the baroque can be shown to have persisted on into literature of the classical generation. For all its rhetorical points and *concetti*, Le Moyne's style conforms to the conventional notion of *sermo gravis*. He mixes themes but treats war, love, and religion always in elevated language. His vocabulary is rich but never descends to the low, nor does he mix high, middle, and low styles. Le Moyne always adheres to the strictest literary decorum. And it is evident that, during the period of revision, from 1653 to 1658, he consciously dampened some of the more baroque or simply archaic elements in his style, that he "classicized" it. At any rate, *Saint Louis* proved to be not sufficiently classical to find favor with Boileau's generation. It was natural for Boileau and his friends to unseat the leading poets of the preceding age, and for the Ancients of the 1670s to attack the Moderns of the 1650s. Less forgivable is the fact that generations of scholars, extending to our own day, persist in seeing the baroque with Boileau's eyes as they see the Middle Ages with Ronsard's.

In many respects, Le Moyne's is a typically Cornelian world (cf. above, pp. 33-36). *Saint Louis* is composed in the grand manner, in a solemn, sublime style, using all the classical figures of rhetoric. In everything he wrote, Le Moyne strove to avoid the trivial and vulgar. Like Corneille, he believed in the values of duty, sacrifice, and chivalry; like Corneille's, his characters shine with glory. These aristocrats are profoundly *généreux* in the Cornelian sense, that is, of noble blood and caste. Their *vertu* can be defined as manliness, grandeur of heart, and the resolution to become and remain a master. They possess a vivid desire to resist the inconstancy of the times, to remain true to the ideals they hold dear. They prove to themselves and to others the law they freely choose. Nothing can prevent a Le Moyne or a Corneille hero from acting—neither memory, prudence, scruples, nor adverse counsel. Totally free, such a man wins our admiration by exercising his will to the utmost. And we admire him for his splendid ardor, for manifesting an almost prelapsarian strength and joy.[37]

I believe that Father Le Moyne reacts against an amorous *galant* current in the 1650s, a *préciosité* and *tendresse* that had infected contemporary French epic and romance and even Corneille's theatre. Curiously, Le Moyne's revulsion from this current parallels that of Boileau. Repudiating Scudéry and Tasso, he seeks to restore an earlier heroic vision of life, now lost. In his poem order triumphs over passion, and heroism over sexual love. Instead of an Alaric or Clovis or Rinaldo feminized within a shady garden, his Lisamante and Belinde are transformed into men. Unlike the author of the *Song of Roland*, Le Moyne does not remove women from his epic; on the contrary, he rehabilitates them by granting them the same martial heroism embodied in their suitors and husbands. Comrades in arms, they join battle side by side in a world of glory.

It is in the nature of his ideals that Le Moyne diverges most from Corneille. The dramatist from Rouen illustrates the last flowering of a feudal mentality, the striving of great aristocrats to defy fate, to exalt their egos at the expense of others, to express

---

[37] It is quite possible that Le Moyne's very notion of heroism is due to the influence of Corneille. See André Stegmann, "L'ambiguïté du concept héroïque dans la littérature morale en France sous Louis XIII," in *Héroïsme et création littéraire sous les règnes d'Henri IV et de Louis XIII*, ed. N. Hepp and G. Livet (Paris, 1974), pp. 29-51, esp. p. 30, n. 3.

their pride, authority, self-assertion, and even rebellion in the face of central authority. In his best known plays erotic love is joined to reason and harmonized with the will; as in courtly romance, love and honor stand together, the one supporting the other, each impossible without the other. In *La Sainte Couronne reconquise*, on the other hand, purified love is rendered subservient to war and religion; if it cannot inspire noble sentiments, it has to be uprooted. Meanwhile, the political and personal ambitions of the great barons are directed against a foreign adversary. Within France, King Louis is an absolute monarch reigning over all, and the greatest of his men, Anjou, Artois, Poitiers, even Bourbon, live only to serve him, to be his sword and shield. Differing from the tradition of epic in Homer and Tasso, Le Moyne suppresses any conflict of authority between the king and his captains. For all their will-power his French, Christian heroes do not act independently from the community or from a higher moral law. Although their lives are their own creation, they fashion them for the purpose of aiding their king and their God.

Above all, Le Moyne's work always contains a supernatural, metaphysical dimension. The interests of the state transcend those of the individual, but God's interests transcend those of the state, and if Louis rules as an absolute king, he does so as God's deputy on earth and in imitation of God's order in the heavens. The ultimate in Le Moyne's world is the after-life. Kings live and rule justly, in order to be seated on an eternal throne in heaven, a crown of laurel or roses on their brows. Since life is threatened by death, permanence by mutability, and reality by appearance, the only truth, being, and constancy are to be found beyond the grave. God is the only register of life, action, energy, and will. Thus, in what he considers to be decadent times, Pierre Le Moyne seeks to restore values in a new heroic synthesis that will combine *virtus* and *pietas*, the beauty of roses and of the stars, that will reconcile the Church and the secular world of Louis XIV's court.

We must never forget that Le Moyne's century represents one of the most fruitful periods of religious activity in all of French history, that the *grand siècle* brought about reform in religious orders, the introduction into France of the discalced Carmelites and the founding of the Oratoire and Saint-Sulpice. This is the age of saints and theologians as well as of the classical theatre and *préciosité*. Pierre Le Moyne belongs to the last generation of baroque religious poets, including Bussières, Martial de Brives, Du Bois Hus, and the Protestant Drelincourt. His is one of the last voices of the Catholic Renaissance. The great themes of the Counter Reformation and of the Jesuit Order are to be found in his work. Le Moyne is a fine poet *because* he belonged to the Society of Jesus and was inspired by the ideals of his order, one of many Jesuit humanists and mystical writers. His *Saint Louis* reflects the ostentatious, ornamental, sensuous, and mystically intolerant Catholicism of his age. He and Tasso are the Western Catholic counterparts of d'Aubigné and Milton. They represent the sublime militant spirit of the Catholic Renaissance (also to be found in Poland, Hungary, and Croatia)[38] which has made a significant moral and esthetic contribution to our civilization.[39]

[38] Waclaw Potocki, *Transakcja Wojny Chocimskiej*; Miclós Zrínyi, *Szigeti veszedelem;* Ivan Gundulić, *Osman*.

[39] Warnke, *Versions of Baroque*, chap. 7, underscores the preeminence of religion as a motivating force and central theme in baroque epic. I should like to add that in this respect the seventeenth century contrasts paradoxically with the Middle Ages, where so many *chansons de geste* and courtly romances are of secular inspiration.

# STANFORD FRENCH AND ITALIAN STUDIES

*Editor: Alphonse Juilland – Stanford University*

1. **Robert Greer Cohn**. *Modes of Art*. An original aesthetics from the author of *L'Oeuvre de Mallarmé*; topics include the image, the symbol, genre, poetic realism, impressionism, creative temper.

2. **Michele Leone**. *L'industria nella letteratura italiana contemporanea*. The first discussion of industrialization in Italian society on the basis of works by Zolla, Vittorini, Bernari, Micheli, Arpino, Bianciardi, Buzzi, Bigiaretti, Calvino, Mastronardi, Ottieri, etc.

3. Edd. **J. Beauroy, M. Bertrand, J. Gargan**. *Popular Culture in France*. Contributions by leading scholars among whom Mandrou, Soriano, Weber, Roubin.

4. **Jacques Beauroy**. *Vin et société à Bergerac du moyen âge aux temps modernes*. An original and remarkable contribution to the history of French vineyards and of the Gascon wine trade; based on private archives.

5. **Alphonse Juilland**. *Structuralist and Transformationalist Morphology*. Confronts the descriptive and explanatory powers of the structuralist and transformational models in morphology.

6. **William Calin**. *Crown, Cross, and 'Fleur-de-lis'*. The first extended modern critical work devoted to Pierre Le Moyne's 'Saint Louis' deals with influence of Tasso, typology, treatment of women, imagery, elements of the baroque, etc.

7. **John C. Lapp**. *The Brazen Tower: Essays on Mythological Imagery in the French Renaissance and Baroque, 1550-1670*. Studies the impact of Greek and Roman mythology on French poetry, particularly on Pontus de Tyard, Du Bellay, Ronsard, D'Aubigné, Tristan l'Hermite, Corneille and La Fontaine.

Available Fall 1977:

8. **Hélène Fredrickson**. *Baudelaire: Héros et Fils. Dualité et Problèmes du Travail dans les Lettres à sa Mère*.

9. **Charles A. Porter**. *Chateaubriand: Composition, Imagination, and Poetry*.